CALL YO A WOLVES FAN?

THE ULTIMATE
WOLVERHAMPTON
WANDERERS
QUIZ BOOK

DEDICATION AND ACKNOWLEDGEMENTS

Firstly, I'd like to thank Michelle Grainger at Pitch Publishing who originally put forward the idea of a series of books on individual clubs. The fact that she is herself a Wolves fan was a factor in my decision to make it an early one, and she has overseen its progress.

Secondly, I would like to thank Andy Howland for his part in reading the manuscript and preparing it for publication.

Thirdly, I have a memory from the mid-1990s teaching at Windsor College every Wednesday. Around five o'clock if Wolves were playing at home a guy called Tars who taught there could be seen racing for his car with his Wolves scarf billowing out behind him as he prepared for the miseries of the M6. I've long since lost touch with him, but after a day's teaching that journey is testament to his support for the club. If you're still out there, well done mate.

RACING POST

CALL YOURSELF A WOLVES FAN?

THE ULTIMATE
WOLVERHAMPTON WANDERERS
QUIZ BOOK

MART MATTHEWS

First published by Pitch Publishing on behalf of Racing Post, 2021

Pitch Publishing

A2 Yeoman Gate

Yeoman Way

Worthing

Sussex

BN13 3QZ

www.pitchpublishing.co.uk

info@pitchpublishing.co.uk

www.racingpost.com/shop

A CIP catalogue record is available for this book
from the British Library.

ISBN 9781839500756

Typesetting and origination by Pitch Publishing
Printed and bound in India by Replika Press Pvt. Ltd.

CONTENTS

INTRODUCTION

Greetings Wolves fans wherever you may have wandered and welcome to what I hope is the most comprehensive quiz on Wolverhampton Wanderers in existence. I'm sure it will stimulate debate between supporters. If you notice a slight leaning towards the 1950s on my part it probably reflects two things. Firstly, that the club enjoyed the greatest period in its history by a very wide margin and secondly that I grew up in that decade and those footballing images at an impressionable age stay with you and shine with a greater intensity than later eras.

I need to say a word about the League Cup, which came into being in the 1960/61 season. Among its many sponsors are five companies involved with drinks. There's an early question. Who are they? To me it has always been the League Cup and always will be whatever transient sponsor it has at any particular time. It is a tedious task each time it crops up to look at who is sponsoring it at that point and is a largely futile act. Therefore, in this quiz it is simply 'the League Cup', end of story.

QUIZ No. 1

ANYTHING GOES - PART 1

1. Who is the odd man out here and why? Neil Emblen, George Saville, Jed Wallace and Andy Keogh

2. In season 1907/08 Wolves were represented by five players who shared a surname with a member of a famous rock group. They were a Beatle, a Rolling Stone and the drummers from Pink Floyd, Dire Straits and Genesis. Who were the five?

3. What links the following Wolves players? Derek Mountfield, Cyril Regis, Andy Gray and Steve Froggatt?

4. Which Wolves player, who shares his full name with a comedian, signed for them in 2013 and has since played for Bradford City, Sheffield United and Wigan Athletic?

5. Which colour has scored for Wolves in an FA Cup Final?

6. Teams with Wanderers in their name have won the FA Cup 13 times. Which two clubs other than Wolves share nine between them?

7. Between 1952/53 and 1959/60 there was only one season when Wolves finished outside the top three in the old First Division. When was it?

8. His name sounds like something a surgeon might ask an assistant to pass him during an operation, and after you had played against him the hospital is most likely where you would find yourself! In ten years at Molineux, before Billy Wright signed him for Arsenal, he played more than 200 times for Wolves. Who was he?

9. Who is the odd man out here and why?
Steven Ward, Steve Kindon, Sam Vokes and Chris Iwolumo.

10. 1983/84 was a terrible season. Wolves didn't win in the league until their 15th game. Some compensation came from the name of the ground where Wolves finally won 3-1. What was it?

QUIZ No. 2

ANYTHING GOES - PART 2

1. Wolverhampton Wanderers have the longest name of any club to have won the FA Cup. Who has the shortest?

2. Who is the only man with a palindromic surname to play for Wolves?

3. The only post-war player to be capped for England while playing for a Welsh club also had a spell at Wolves during his career. Who is he?

4. Which Wolves winger who represented the club between 1959 and 1964 later moved to America to manage Seattle Sounders after ending his career with two medals for winning the league twice with another club?

5. Cliff Durandt, Des Horne and Eddie Stuart between them played over 400 games for Wolves in the 1950s and 1960s. How are they linked?

6. What was extremely rare about the old Division One league programme for Saturday, 10 December 1955 when Wolves beat Burnley 3-1 at Molineux?

7. Wath Wanderers were an important nursery club for Wolves, particularly in the 1940s and 1950s. In which county could they be found?

8. A cross between a Rolling Stone and a famous London Street, he came to Molineux from Notts County in 1987, played exactly 200 games in all competitions for the club, before leaving for Birmingham City in 1993. Who was he?

9. In 1895/96, Wolves registered their lowest-ever number of draws in a season in the Football League. How many?

10. A cross between an assassinated president and the building he lived in, he played over 150 League games for Wolves in the first seven years of the 20th century. Who was he?

QUIZ No. 3

ANYTHING GOES - PART 3

1. On 14 September 2019, Wolves were beaten 5-2 at Molineux by Chelsea. Which visiting player got three goals for his own team and one for Wolves into the bargain?

2. These two Wolves players both have seven letters in their surnames, six of them being the same and in the right order. They only differ from each other in the second letter of their names. One of them was a member of the Wolves team that won the FA Cup in 1960, while the other was a popular goalkeeper from a later time. Who are the two men?

3. Who is the only country to have a spell as chairman of Wolverhampton Wanderers?

4. Whose 89th minute winner against Manchester City at Molineux on 27 December 2019 was a very acceptable late Christmas bonus?

5. Which flamboyant Wolves player won the 'Best dressed man of the year' award back in the day?

6. Which member of Wolves' League Cup-winning team of 1974 came to the club from Manchester City, the side that Wolves beat in that final?

7. What is the link between the following two players who were members of teams that opposed Wolves in cup finals? The first played right-back for Leicester City against Wolves in the 1949 FA Cup Final, while the second played for Spurs against Wolves in the two-leg UEFA Cup Final of 1972.

8. When Wolves recorded their biggest league win by beating Leicester City 10-1 on 15 April 1938, the visitors' consolation goal was scored via an own goal by a Wolves player. Who scored it?

9. Who scored his first goal for Wolves in a 2-0 home win over Crystal Palace on 20 July 2020?

10. One member of the Wolves side that won the League Cup in 1980 by beating Nottingham Forest had a surname that was shared by a player on the opposing team that day. What was that surname?

QUIZ No. 4

APPEARANCES

1. Who is the only player in the history of the club to make more than 500 league appearances for them?

2. In season 1987/88, Wolves played 61 games in all competitions, creating a new club record. Which two men appeared in all 61 games?

3. Season 1953/54 was the only one between the resumption of league football after the war and the 1960s where a Wolves player appeared in every game for the club. Which forward made all 42 games that season?

4. Billy Wright was capped for England 105 times while with Wolves. No other Wolves player has reached even 50. True or false?

5. Which Wolves defender's time at Molineux spanned three decades, beginning in 1965 and ending with a move to Sheffield United in 1981? By the time he left, he had made just over 500 appearances in all competitions for the club.

6. Did those Wolves favourites Derek Dougan and John Richards between them start under or over 600 league games for the club?

7. Who played in all 42 league games for Wolves when they finished runners-up in the old First Division in the last completed season before World War Two of 1938/39?

8. Who made 107 league appearances for Wolves from 1986 to 1990 but had previously made over 500 for another club not a million miles away?

9. Which Wolves player started all 38 league games in the club's first season back in the big time of 2018/19?

10. In the 1920s, Noel George played 126 consecutive games in the Wolves goal. Which goalkeeper broke his record for Wolves in September 1973?

QUIZ No. 5

ATTENDANCES

1. Wolves have appeared in eight FA Cup finals. When was the only occasion that the official crowd was in six figures?

2. A crowd of 2,500 turned up at Wolves' first league game on 8 September 1888 when they entertained which club in a 1-1 draw?

3. Outside of an FA Cup Final, the first 20,000 crowd to watch Wolves play came to an away game on Boxing Day 1891 against which northern club?

4. Wolves have figured as the away side in the attendance records at a number of grounds. One such record came in the fourth-round FA Cup tie on 2 February 1952 at which northern ground, where 61,905 fans were crammed in ?

5. How many attended when Wolves won the FA Cup for the first time in 1893? Was it 25,000, 35,000 , 45,000 or 55,000?

6. Wolves set the record for an Old Trafford attendance in an FA Cup semi-final on that ground on 25 March 1939 with a figure of 76,962. Wolves were also the visitors when their semi-final opponents on that day broke their own ground record on 20 February 1937. Who were they?

7. Which now defunct Midlands ground had its record crowd of 51,455 when Wolves were their visitors for a Division Two game on 29 April 1967?

8. Which Lancastrian ground's attendance record was set at 38,098 when Wolves came to town on 17 September 1955?

9. On which northern ground did Wolves attract a crowd of 72,569 for an FA Cup fourth-round replay on 31 January 1948?

10. Which London ground that no longer exists had 67,311 supporters inside it for the visit of Wolves for a league game on 4 September 1937?

QUIZ No. 6

AWAY FROM MOLINEUX

Name the following Wolves men who played in cup finals for other clubs:

1. He was with Wolves between 1991 and 1994 after signing from Aston Villa. While with Everton, he had appeared in three successive FA Cup finals in the mid-1980s.

2. This Welsh international goalkeeper joined Wolves in 1937 and played for them through the war years before joining Liverpool in time to play for them against Arsenal in the 1950 FA Cup Final.

3. Before joining Wolves in the following season, he had played for Manchester United against Bolton Wanderers in their losing FA Cup Final of 1958.

4. Previously he was a member of the Crystal Palace team that lost to Manchester United after a replay in the 1990 FA Cup Final and he joined Wolves in 1993.

5. A surprise choice up front for Leicester City in the 1961 FA Cup Final against Spurs, he joined Wolves from Carlisle United in 1964 before returning to that club in 1967.

6. At Wolves in the mid-1970s, he had previously been a member of Arsenal's 'double'-winning side of 1970/71.

7. He was an unused substitute for Coventry City when they beat Spurs in the 1987 FA Cup Final before finally winning the cup in 1991 when Spurs beat Forest. He came to Molineux from Ipswich in 1997.

8. Signed for Wolves from junior football after the war, he spent a decade at Molineux before moving to Aston Villa in 1956. A year later, he took part in their FA Cup Final win over Manchester United.

9. He joined Wolves from school in 1969 before moving on to Arsenal in 1977. Two years later, he experienced the joy of scoring the winning goal in an FA Cup Final against Manchester United.

10. Two goalkeepers to end with whose names begin with the same letter. The first spent eight years at Molineux as understudy to Bert Williams before moving to Aston Villa in time to win the FA Cup with them in 1957. The second was with Wolves from 1954 to 1961 before also leaving to join Aston Villa where he straight away won a League Cup winner's medal with that club, playing in one of the two legs of the final against Rotherham United.

QUIZ No. 7

CAPITAL CITIES

1. When Wolves famously entertained clubs from Hungary and the Soviet Union under the Molineux lights in the mid-1950s, one of the numerous headlines was 'Wonderful, wonderful Wolverhampton'. This was a corruption of a popular song of the time about a capital city. Which one? It might help you to know that Steve Bull's first game outside Britain for England came as a substitute in this same city.

2. Which is the only capital city in which Wolves have played a European final?

3. In which European capital did Wolves draw 1-1 on 11 November 1959 in the European Cup?

4. Which is the only capital city in which Wolves have scored nine goals in a game?

5. When England beat Chile 2-0 in the World Cup on 25 June 1950, Wolves provided three players for the national team. They were Bert Williams, Billy Wright and Jimmy Mullen. In which capital city was the match played?

6. Wolves' popular winger Norman Deeley played just twice for England, both times away from home and both times in a capital city. He made his debut in a 2-0 defeat to Brazil in Rio. In his second match, they lost again, this time by 4-1. In which capital city did this take place?

7. In which capital city did Bert Williams make his England debut in a 3-1 win on 22 May 1949?

8. In which capital city did Wolves play their first match in the European Cup Winners' Cup, going down 2-0 in a first-leg tie on 12 October 1960?

9. Billy Wright's 50th cap for England came in a 2-1 defeat on 31 May 1953 in which capital city?

10. On 20 May 1956, Wolves forward Dennis Wilshaw scored in England's 5-1 win in which capital city? If it helps, Mixu Paatelainen was born there.

QUIZ No.8

CHRISTMAS CRACKERS

1. Wolves met the same club at Molineux two Boxing Days running in the First Division in 1996 and 1997, winning both matches by 3-1 and 1-0. Who were their visitors who once shared Wolves' colours?

2. Boxing Day of 1963 remains legendary because 66 goals were scored in the ten top-flight games that day, a number highly unlikely to ever be beaten. Wolves entertained Aston Villa that day at Molineux. What was the outcome?

3. On Boxing Day of 2018, who levelled for Wolves in the 85th minute of their game at Craven Cottage against Fulham?

4. Wolves were away on Boxing Day four years in a row between 1983 and 1986. They played at Ipswich Town, Shrewsbury Town, Notts County and Hereford United. All of the games ended the same way. Did Wolves win all four, draw all four or lose all four?

5. Which Midlands club did Wolves meet at Christmas three years in a row in 1971, 1972 and 1973, twice away and once at Molineux, winning two and drawing the other?

6. Wolves met Derby County on Christmas Eve in 1966. Hatton, Wharton and McIlmoyle were all among the scorers in a festive treat for 24,378 inside Molineux. By what score did Wolves win the game?

7. In which post-war season was the weather so severe for such a long time that Wolves played no Yuletide fixtures? In fact, Wolves drew 3-3 at Manchester City on 15 December and their next match took place on 19 January. The long wait ended, as such things tend to, with a 0-0 draw at home to Sheffield United.

8. In which post-war season did Wolves play their last game on Christmas Day? It was a 3-1 home defeat against Everton.

9. Which northern club did Wolves beat 7-0 at Molineux on Boxing Day 1931?

10. Which team have Wolves met the most times over the Christmas period?

QUIZ No. 9

CRAZY DAYS

1. On 5 September 1959, Wolves were involved in a ten-goal thriller at Maine Road against Manchester City. What was the score?

2. On 27 March 1965, Wolves came out on the wrong side of an 11-goal bonanza at White Hart Lane against Spurs. What was the score?

3. Which London club shared eight goals with Wolves at Molineux in a 4-4 draw in the 2016/17 season?

4. The first time Wolves won by this score was in 1900 against Derby County. They repeated the feat against Luton Town in 1956 and also against Chelsea in 1962. What was the score?

5. Twice in the year of 1960, but in different seasons, Wolves drew away 4-4. One game was in London while the other took place in the North East. Which two clubs did they entertain the crowds with?

6. 6-4 is a very rare scoreline, but Wolves have twice beaten one Yorkshire club 6-4 at Molineux, firstly in 1933 and then again in 1955. Who were their opponents?

7. As rare as it is, Wolves have also beaten a London club 6-4 at Molineux on 26 April 1947. Which one?

8. Which club from Lancashire beat Wolves 5-4 twice between 1928 and 1930?

9. Which major rival of Wolves at the time did they both beat 6-2 and lose to 6-2 at Molineux between 1947 and 1952?

10. On 27 October 1962, Wolves visited Highbury to play Arsenal and the 43,000 crowd were treated to a nine-goal thriller. What was the score?

QUIZ No. 10

CRYPTIC WOLVES - PART 1

You are given the number of league games played, the dates of their time at Molineux and a cryptic clue.

Can you identify the players?

1. Sounds like he should be playing for Sheffield United! – 107 games between 1992 and 1995.

2. This is not the condition you want to find the answer to the first question in – 58 games between 1908 and 1912.

3. Actor who played the doctor who wanted his sausages in *Fawlty Towers* – 416 games between 1970–84 and 1985–87.

4. Goalkeeper found in the Lake District –147 games between 1986 and 1990.

5. Combination of a season of the year and a Liberal Party leader – 35 games between 1939 and 1950.

6. I think he wore the customary black shorts rather than blue jeans, but he certainly sounds unearthly! – 287 games between 1987 and 1997.

7. Like The Beatles song on the *White Album*, he was 'Bungalow Bill' – 344 games between 1941 and 1957.

8. World Cup winner of 1966 is used to draw out the Premium Bond winners – 74 games between 1965 and 1968.

9. Shy Shilling! – 43 games between 1979 and 1984.

10. Didn't stay long, but had risen from the dead to be here! – nine games between 1961 and 1962.

QUIZ No. 11

CRYPTIC WOLVES - PART 2

You are given the number of league games played, the dates of their time at Molineux and a cryptic clue.

Can you identify the players?

1. Male cat at Christmas – 33 games between 1911 and 1913.

2. You don't want defenders at the club who are like this Californian airport – 61 games between 1929 and 1931.

3. Water biscuit – 237 games between 1975 and 1982.

4. *Goon Show* character found in Lancashire – 36 games between 1896 and 1898.

5. Combination of World Cup-winning manager and a chess piece – 357 games between 1906 and 1920.

6. He had the perfect name for a Wolves player – 28 games between 1994 and 1995.

7. Combination of Wolves' goalkeeper in the 1921 FA Cup Final and a fruit – 124 games between 1975 and 1982.

8. Combination of a Beatle and a railway timetable – 200 games between 1977 and 1984.

9. The first black man to be featured in a Broadway revue, he inspired a Duke Ellington track in 1940 – 381 games between 1945 and 1957.

10. Combination of a Biblical character, a Puerto Rican city and a major winning golfer – four games in 1997/98.

QUIZ No. 12

DYNAMIC DUOS

Each one of the 40 sets of names that may be a famous person, a famous duo, phrase or product, contains at least one Wolves player. One of the four duos in each set contains two Wolves players. Can you identify it in each case? For example, some that I had to leave out that do contain two Wolves players are: Pope Francis, Black and White, Westwood and Rose, James Mason, Knight and Bishop, and Brown and Blair.

1. (a) North and South (b) Holmes and Watson (c) King and Queen
    (d) Long and Short

2. (a) Homer Simpson (b) Lester Piggott (c) Graham Greene
    (d) Dudley Moore

3. (a) Jagger and Richards (b) Mason Dixon (c) Cannon and Ball
    (d) Cock and Bull

4. (a) Adam Scott (b) Duncan Edwards (c) Stanley Matthews
    (d) Godfrey Evans

5. (a) Barker and Corbett (b) Flanagan and Allen (c) Heath and
    Wilson, (d) Pearl and Dean

6. (a) Root and Branch (b) Mills and Boon (c) Crabtree and Evelyn (d)
    Holland and Barrett

7. (a) Gold and Silver (b) March and May (c) Crosse and Blackwell
    (d) Preston and Sunderland

8. (a) Hatfield and McCoy (b) Large and Small (c) Young and Old
    (d) Goodman and Crook

9. (a) Thorpe Park (b) Campbell and McDonald (c) Nightingale and
    Pheasant (d) Farmer Giles

10. (a) George Harrison (b) Power Walker (c) Shackleton and Scott
    (d) Nixon and Trump

QUIZ No. 13

FA CUP FINALS

Wolves have contested FA Cup finals in 1889, 1893, 1896, 1908, 1921, 1939, 1949 and 1960.

1. Who are the only team that by beating Wolves in the FA Cup Final completed the coveted league and cup double?

2. Only two men have scored more than once in an FA Cup Final for Wolves, the first in 1949 and the second in 1960. Who are the two players?

3. What was it about the four goals scored when Wolves beat Newcastle United 3-1 in the 1908 FA Cup Final that made it unique?

4. Wolves were strong favourites to lift the FA Cup in 1939 when they were beaten 4-1 on the day by Portsmouth. Who scored Wolves' consolation goal?

5. In the 1960 FA Cup Final against Blackburn Rovers, manager Stan Cullis left out inside-forward Bobby Mason, who had played in 37 league games that season, replacing him with a youngster who had played just four. Who was he?

6. Of the eight FA Cup finals that Wolves have played in, which was the only one where they had knocked out both Everton and Liverpool to get there?

7. No member of the Wolves side that won the FA Cup in 1949 played in the 1960 FA Cup Final when they won it again. True or false?

8. Wolves captain in the 1893 FA Cup Final against Everton was also the scorer of their winning goal in a 1-0 win. Sadly, he died at the age of 29. Who was he?

9. Which future England manager was injured and unable to play for Leicester against Wolves in the 1949 FA Cup Final?

10. Wolves have contested one FA Cup Final where neither they nor their opponents were in the top flight of English football. Which of the eight finals was it?

QUIZ No. 14

FANS

1. Which member of Monty Python is a Wolves fan?

2. Which female commentator and radio and TV presenter is a Wolves fan?

3. In the Edwardian era, England's greatest composer could often be seen at Molineux. Who was he?

4. Which member of Led Zeppelin was a Wolves fan from the time he was taken as a young boy to see Wolves playing foreign opposition under the Molineux lights in the 1950s?

5. How many fans did Wolves take to Anfield for their FA Cup fourth-round tie against Liverpool in 2017? They returned happy because Wolves did them proud with a 2-1 win.

6. 'Wolfie' the Wolves mascot got himself into a spot of bother after an incident involving one of the three little pigs! On what ground did all this excitement take place?

7. What is the name of the Asian fans' group that supports Wolves?

8. Which TV presenter, primarily in motorsport, is a keen Wolves fan?

9. Who started the fanzine *A load of Bull* in 1989 before handing over the editorship to Charles Ross in 1993?

10. Which two other clubs at that time had a fanzine with 'Bull' in the title?

QUIZ No. 15

FIRSTS AND LASTS

1. What was unusual about Wolves' first goal in the Football League against Aston Villa in a 1-1 draw on 8 September 1888?

2. Who scored Wolves' first Division Two goal on 1 September 1906 in a 1-1 home draw with Hull City after the Wanderers' relegation from the top flight the previous season?

3. Whose brace of goals in a 2-0 win at Leicester on 4 May 1939, were the last Wolves goals of the last completed league season before World War Two?

4. When Wolves won the league for the first time in 1953/54, their first and last goals of the season were scored by the same player. Who was he?

5. When Wolves won the League Cup in 1980, they started out on their journey with a 1-1 draw at Burnley on 28 August 1979. Who scored their goal?

6. Who got Wolves' last goal of the 20th century in a 1-0 home win over Norwich City on 28 December 1999?

7. Who scored their first goal of the new century six days later in a 1-1 draw at Blackburn?

8. Who scored Wolves' first FA Cup goal of the new century in a 1-1 draw at Sheffield Wednesday on 8 January 2000?

9. Who, in the late 1980s, scored Wolves' last-ever goal at the old Wembley Stadium?

10. It was over a decade before Wolves broke their duck by scoring at the new Wembley and it happened on a day that ended in great disappointment. Who scored that first Wolves goal at the new place?

QUIZ No. 16

GOALKEEPERS - PART 1

1. Wolves were his first club in 1983 and he played in 63 league games for them. He was best known later for winning a Premier League title in 1995 with Blackburn Rovers. Who was he?

2. His clubs run into double figures and he was known for performing calisthenics in his goalmouth before games. His Wolves career comprised 74 league games between 1982 and 1984 before his transfer to Sheffield United via a short loan spell at Derby County. Who was he?

3. In 1993 he played four league games between the posts for Wolves, but he is more well known for saving a penalty in an FA Cup Final in 1988 and for dropping a jar of mayonnaise on his toe, though not at the same time. Who was he?

4. This Scottish goalkeeper came from Millwall in 1956 and eventually made the position his own with over 200 games to his credit, winning both the League title and the FA Cup while at Molineux. Who was he?

5. He only turned out for the Wolves eight times in the league between 1961 and 1965 before leaving to join Chelsea. However, he returned to be Wolves' caretaker manager for a short time in the troubled years of the mid-1980s. Who was he?

6. He first played for Chester City in 1987. After seven games for Wolves he moved on to Preston North End for a couple of games before finally settling at Molineux to such an extent that he went on to break the appearance record for a goalkeeper at the club. Who was he?

7. He came from Welsh club Newport County in 1986 and left to join another in Swansea City in 1990. Between these times he managed 147 league games guarding the Wolves net. Who was he?

8. He made over 300 appearances in the league for Wolves from the early 1960s to the late 1970s, playing in both legs of the 1972 UEFA Cup Final versus Spurs. Who was he?

9. Between 1977 and 1984 he played exactly 200 league games for Wolves after signing from Blackburn Rovers. Eventually, he tried his luck with Vancouver Whitecaps in Canada. Who was he?

10. This England international, who joined Wolves in 1889, was sacked by the club in 1894 for inciting players to become unionised, but came back the following year for a further stint, and played over 150 times in all competitions for the club. Who was he?

QUIZ No. 17

GOALKEEPERS - PART 2

1. He played in goal for Wolves in the 1908 FA Cup Final before a move to Spurs in 1911 after a total of 142 games for the club. Who was he?

2. Bert Williams was widely regarded as the greatest goalkeeper in the club's history and I certainly wouldn't argue against that view. How many England caps did he win between 1949 and 1956 in the days before they started dishing them out like confetti?

3. Which Merseysider was at Wolves from 1957 onwards but didn't make his debut until the 1961/62 season, by which time the club was in decline? That didn't stop him from making 173 appearances in all competitions, he just had more shots to stop for his money! On the brighter side, he was a member of their promotion-winning team of 1966/67 before joining Cardiff City in 1968.

4. In this century, Wolves have experienced the very unusual situation of having two goalkeepers with the same surname at the club at the same time. Their first names also begin with the same letter. Who are they?

5. Which Wolves goalkeeper has won the most international caps in his overall career?

6. Which goalkeeper came to Wolves from Aston Villa in 1999 and played over 200 games for the Wanderers before joining Cardiff City in 2007?

7. Which Wolves goalkeeper, before he came to Molineux, was the first goalkeeper to be used as a substitute in an FA Cup Final when he replaced the injured Antti Niemi in the 66th minute of the 2003 final while playing for Southampton against Arsenal?

8. Which Wolves goalkeeper was so unlucky with injuries that he was forced to retire at the age of 29 after a loan spell at Hereford United and now works for Sky Sports?

9. Which goalkeeper played over 200 times for Wolves in all competitions between 2005 and 2017 when he had to retire after being diagnosed with a serious illness?

10. Who played in goal for Wolves in the 1921 FA Cup Final against Spurs?

QUIZ No. 18

HAT-TRICKS - PART 1

1. Who, on 6 November 1999, scored Wolves' last hat-trick of the 20th century in a 3-0 win over Grimsby Town at Molineux?

2. 6 November again! Who on that date in 1998 grabbed four goals in a 6-1 win at Bristol City?

3. If you are going to score a hat-trick for Wolves it boosts the status of the achievement if it comes against a rival club. Two players with the same surname did this, the first on his debut against Birmingham City on 27 September 1992 in a 4-0 win. The second came against West Brom on 15 September 1996 in a 4-2 win. Who were the two players?

4. In the 1952/53 season, Wolves hammered both Manchester clubs at Molineux, beating United 6-2 and City 7-2. Who scored a hat-trick in both games?

5. Which Wolves midfielder scored a rare hat-trick of headers against Sunderland at Molineux on 20 April 1965 in a 3-0 win?

6. Wolves had three hat-tricks to their name in the 1957/58 season, two in the league against Birmingham City and Nottingham Forest and one in the FA Cup against Darlington. One man was responsible for all three. Who was he?

7. Who scored a hat-trick for Wolves on the last day of the 1955/56 season at Sheffield United in a 3-3 draw and followed it up with another the next season when he got four in a 5-2 win over Arsenal on 10 November 1956?

8. Who is the only player to score a hat-trick for Wolves either side of World War Two?

9. Add two letters to the surname of the scorer of three hat-tricks for Wolves in the 1930s and produce the surname of a player who scored seven hat-tricks for the club in the 1920s. Who are the two players?

10. Normally this bird gets shot at, but on this occasion he was doing the shooting, bagging three against Newcastle United on 10 March 1902 in a 3-0 win. Who was he?

HAT-TRICKS – PART 2

1. Who scored a phenomenal 16 hat-tricks for Wolves between 1929 and 1935?

2. Hat-tricks against West Brom are always a welcome sight and the next three questions concern those happy events. Firstly, which winger scored the three goals that beat the Albion at Molineux on 2 December 1950?

3. Another winger got in on the act in a 5-2 win over West Brom on 21 March 1959. Who was he?

4. It was yet another winger who got a hat-trick on 16 March 1963 when Wolves really went into overdrive against the old enemy, beating them 7-0 at Molineux. What was his name?

5. Who scored a hat-trick in a 4-1 win over Charlton Athletic in the FA Cup fifth round on 19 February 1955?

6. He came from Feyenoord in 1994 and went back there before 1995 was out, scoring just five goals for Wolves. However, three of the five came in the same game, a 4-2 win at Port Vale on 25 February 1995. Who was he?

7. Which Wolves player scored a hat-trick against Nottingham Forest on 3 April 1971 in a Molineux encounter that ended in a 4-0 win for the home side?

8. Who became Wolves' first scorer of a hat-trick in a League Cup tie when Barnet were beaten 5-0 at Molineux on 18 August 1998?

9. Hat-tricks were harder to find in our current century. Who got one for Wolves in a ten-goal thriller at home to Rotherham in April 2014?

10. Who scored Wolves' first hat-trick of the 1970s when they beat Manchester United 3-2 at Molineux on 3 October 1970?

QUIZ No. 20

HORRIBLE HAMMERINGS

These are the games the fans would like to forget, but some of them linger in the memory:

1. Which London club scored five times at home and away to Wolves in the 2003/04 season?

2. The supporters of which seaside-town club went home happy on 20 January 1962 after their team had beaten Wolves 7-2 in the league? The only consolation for Wolves fans was the fact that it was witnessed by the lowest crowd to watch Wolves that season, just 13,140.

3. Wolves have never before or since experienced so many hidings on one ground in such a short space of time as what befell them in the years leading up to World War Two. They conceded 22 goals in five seasons there, and previous to this period they also lost 7-1 at home to them on bonfire night in 1932. Which club was such an inhospitable host?

4. Which club from the North East beat Wolves 7-2 in a league game in 1901, and then five years later in 1906 did it again?

5. It was in the third season of the league that Wolves first conceded nine goals in a game, going down 9-0 away to which Midlands club on 10 January 1891?

6. Just before World War One, on 6 December 1913, Hull City walloped Wolves 7-1 and then just after the war, on 27 December 1919, they hammered them again in a match that produced 13 goals in a league record for a game Wolves were involved in. By what score did Wolves lose?

7. The club that eventually became Manchester United inflicted a 10-1 defeat on Wolves on 15 October 1892. Who were they?

8. This team has twice scored six goals against Wolves at Molineux, firstly in the 1976/77 season and again, 30 years later, in 2006/07. For good measure they also beat Wolves 9-3 on 18 September 1965, this time on their own ground. Who were they?

9. Which London club beat Wolves 7-0 in a league game on 4 February 1928 in the capital?

10. Two trips to the North East ended badly for Wolves. The first, on 11 November 1905, ended up 8-0 to the home side, with the second, on 9 February 1929, being slightly kinder to Wolves who went down 8-3. Which two clubs inflicted the damage?

QUIZ No. 21

INTERNATIONALS - ENGLAND

1. When England beat Scotland 7-2 at Wembley in 1955, which Wolves player grabbed four of them?

2. Two Wolves wingers, Johnny Hancocks and Alan Hinton, played for England the same number of times. How many times?

3. Which Wolves player obtained his sole England cap while with the club in 2011?

4. Which Wolves inside-forward found the net twice in his seven appearances for England between 1958 and 1960?

5. Against which country in a match that England won 8-1 did Billy Wright gain his 105th and final cap?

6. Which Wolves player with 49 caps to his name was England's top goalscorer in the World Cup in Chile in 1962?

7. Which Wolves forward was capped eight times by England in 1964 and 1965?

8. Two Wolves forwards, the first in 1963 and the second a decade later, both gained one precious England cap. Who were the two men?

9. Who was the only Wolves player to be capped by England in both the 1980s and the 1990s?

10. Which Wolves player who was 'Footballer of the Year' in 1960 won a dozen England caps during his career?

QUIZ No. 22

INTERNATIONALS - SCOTLAND AND WALES

1. Christophe Berra was capped 41 times by Scotland between 2008 and 2018. Hearts accounted for some of his caps, but which English club besides Wolves was he capped with?

2. Which central defender was capped five times for Wales between 1979 and 1983 while with Wolves and Stoke City?

3. Which Scottish international joined Wolves from Sheffield Wednesday before leaving for Manchester United in 1974?

4. Which two post-war Wolves goalkeepers have played nearly 150 games for Wales between them?

5. Which Wolves defender, who turned out over 300 times for the club, was capped nine times by Scotland between 1971 and 1975?

6. Which Wolves forward began his Welsh international career when with the club in 2008 and has since, with Burnley and Stoke City, gone on to make over 60 appearances for his country?

7. Between 2008 and 2020 he has played more than 30 times up front for Scotland while with five different clubs, Wolves being the third of the five. Who is he?

8. He started out winning caps for Wales while at Luton Town, won some more at Molineux, and some more at Reading, amassing 43 in all between 2007 and 2018. Who was he?

9. Perhaps this Anglo-Scot deserved more than his 20 Scottish caps leading the attack while with Aston Villa, Wolves and Everton between 1976 and 1985. Who was he?

10. Well-travelled Welsh internationals Sam Ricketts and Carl Robinson were both capped while at Wolves this century. What else links them?

QUIZ No. 23

INTERNATIONALS - THE TWO IRELANDS

1. Which Wolves midfielder played 18 times for Northern Ireland between 1988 and 1997?

2. Which Wolves player appeared on five occasions for the Republic of Ireland in 2007/08?

3. Which Wolves forward, who came to the club from Manchester United, played nine games for Northern Ireland between 2010 and 2012?

4. Which Wolves player joined the club after spells at Oxford United and Walsall, and was capped 18 times for the Republic of Ireland between 1970 and 1980?

5. Which Wolves defender managed three caps for Northern Ireland in 2005 and shares a surname with a Scottish football club?

6. Which Wolves defender who came from Luton Town took the field for the Republic of Ireland on eight occasions between 2009 and 2011?

7. This larger-than-life character's international career for Northern Ireland spanned three decades and five clubs and his 43 caps brought him eight goals between 1958 and 1973. Who was this Wolves favourite?

8. Which Wolves defender won two caps for the Republic of Ireland in 1978?

9. Which left-winger who had joined Wolves from Aston Villa gained 34 Northern Ireland caps between 1954 and 1962?

10. Which feisty midfielder collected 39 Republic of Ireland caps between 2007 and 2012 while playing for Reading, Hull City and Wolves?

INTERNATIONALS - OTHER COUNTRIES

These Wolves players have all been capped by their countries. You are given their names and the year they joined the club. Can you name the countries they represented?

1. Jaoa Moutinho – 2018

2. Raul Jimenez – 2018

3. Ricki Herbert – 1984

4. Leander Dendoncker – 2018

5. Bjorn Sigurdarson – 2012

6. Nenad Milijas – 2009

7. Seyi Olofinjana – 2004

8. Ki-Hyeon Seol – 2004

9. Haavard Flo – 1999

10. Steve Corica – 1996

QUIZ No. 25

LEAGUE CUP FINALS

1. On the only two occasions that Wolves have contested a League Cup Final they have returned to Molineux with the trophy. 1974 and 1980 were the years involved. Who were the only two men to score in both of those competitions?

2. Who had to leave the field due to injury in the 1974 final against Manchester City, and who replaced him?

3. In that final, the Wolves team contained a player who would go on to score a goal for another club in an FA Cup Final, and the Manchester City team contained a player who already had scored for a different club in an FA Cup Final. Who are the two players?

4. Gary Pierce performed magnificently in the Wolves goal that day, but only got his chance due to an injury to which Wolves goalkeeper?

5. When Wolves won the trophy again in 1980, it deprived Nottingham Forest of three successive wins in the competition. The goal that put paid to them was a simple tap in for Andy Gray after a mix up at the back between two Forest players. Who were they?

6. Which veteran defender played a stormer at the heart of the Wolves defence that day and won the 'Man of the Match' award into the bargain?

7. When Wolves beat Manchester City in the 1974 final, who was their captain?

8. Wolves played a total of 19 matches to win these League Cups and lost just one of them, in the first leg of the semi-final in 1980. Who beat them?

9. On the way to Wembley in 1980, Wolves knocked out QPR 1-0 at Molineux in the fourth round after a 1-1 draw at Loftus Road. Who got the winner in the replay?

10. On their way to the 1974 final, Wolves disposed of Halifax Town, Tranmere Rovers and Exeter City in the early rounds of the competition. Who was the only player to score in the 3-0 win at Halifax, the 2-1 replay win over Tranmere and the 5-1 home win over Exeter?

QUIZ No. 26

LEGENDS No. 1 - STEVE BULL

1. Steve Bull's first goal for Wolves came in an away tie in the Freight Rover Trophy on 2 December 1986. Which club lost 1-0?

2. By a strange coincidence, the side he scored his first league goal for Wolves against in front of 1,689 spectators on 13 December 1986 was also the one Wolves were playing against when he scored his first Wolves hat-trick at Molineux on the final day of that season. Who were they?

3. While on the subject of hat-tricks, Bully scored just one in the FA Cup for Wolves. It came on 14 November 1987 in a 5-1 first-round win against which club?

4. Which Midlands club did he score against in more than one FA Cup tie?

5. In the same vein, there was just one club, also from the Midlands, that he scored against in more than one League Cup tie. Who are they?

6. His Molineux debut was an inauspicious affair, with Wolves losing 3-0 on 22 November 1986. Which Welsh club did the damage?

7. On 27 May 1989, Steve Bull made his England debut, scoring one of their goals in a 2-0 win. Who were England playing and on which ground was the match held?

8. For how many successive seasons was Steve Bull the leading scorer for Wolves?

9. On 18 February 1998, he got the winning goal at Molineux. It was a bit more special than usual as it was his 300th for Wolves. Which Yorkshire club did he score it against?

10. Which club came to Wolverhampton to provide the opposition for his well-earned testimonial in 1996?

QUIZ No. 27

LEGENDS No. 2 - STAN CULLIS

1. As a player, Stan Cullis made 171 appearances in league and cup for Wolves. How many goals did he score?

2. If you add his games as a player to those as a manager, you get an impressive figure that reflects his selfless commitment to the club. Is that figure 850, 900, 950 or 1,000?

3. 31 May 1947 was almost certainly Stan's worst day in football. It was his final game for Wolves. A win that day in their last game of the season would give Wolves the league title for the first time in their history. A draw against visitors Liverpool would almost certainly give them the title – as Liverpool and Stoke both trailed Wanderers by a point and the Potters had a much inferior goal average. Wolves lost 2-1, and Liverpool's second goal that came from a run from the centre circle could have been prevented if Stan had committed a 'professional foul'. But that wasn't in his make -up. The man who scored the goal that turned out to give Liverpool the title later became immortalised on the cover of *Sergeant Pepper's Lonely Hearts Club Band* by the Beatles. Who was he?

4. After his retirement, he went to Scandinavia for a short period as a coach. In which country?

5. When Stan came back, he worked as assistant to which Wolves manager before taking over in 1948?

6. When Stan Cullis took on the Wolves job, he quickly developed an indomitable spirit in the side and a style of play that did not sit well with the purists. What did his detractors label this style of play?

7. Stan Cullis won more than twice as many league games as he lost as a Wolves manager. True or false?

8. Stan, after recovering from illness in 1964, was given the sack by Wolves chairman John Ireland in a move that shocked the town rigid. Who replaced him?

9. Which other club did Stan Cullis manage?

10. Under his management, Wolves scored an incredible number of league goals in the four successive seasons from 1957 to 1961. Was this total 322, 372, 422 or 472?

QUIZ No. 28

LEGENDS No. 3 - DEREK DOUGAN

1. At which club did Derek Dougan begin his career in the Football League after arriving from Ireland in 1957?

2. Many Wolves fans know that he played for Blackburn Rovers against Wolves in the 1960 FA Cup Final after getting the two semi-final goals against Sheffield Wednesday that took Rovers to Wembley that year. Apart from his lacklustre display and the suspicion that he should not have played while he was carrying an injury, why else might Blackburn fans have been annoyed with him?

3. He scored two hat-tricks in the league for Wolves against another Midlands club. Which one?

4. He managed just two more league hat-tricks for Wolves against which two clubs, one of which shares Wolves' colours?

5. How many caps did he receive for Northern Ireland?

6. Which club sold him to Wolves?

7. Which club did he play for in the Third Division?

8. He scored more league goals for Wolves than for all his five other clubs put together. True or false?

9. Inside six days in October 1974, he scored his last league goal and his last European goal for Wolves. Who were their opponents, one from the North East and the other from Portugal?

10. After his retirement in 1974, Dougan came back to Wolves between 1982 and 1986 in what capacity?

QUIZ No. 29

LEGENDS No. 4 - RON FLOWERS

1. Ron was born near this Yorkshire town, was briefly on their books and both his brother John and uncle George played for them in the league. What town was it?

2. Why was Ron's debut at home to Blackpool on 20 September 1952 a bittersweet affair?

3. As an attacking wing-half, he scored 33 times in his 467 league games. On three occasions he found the net twice in a match. Burnley and West Ham were the victims on two of those occasions, but which London club were involved in the third game?

4. On 3 October 1962, at Hillsborough, Ron Flowers scored from the penalty spot for England in a 1-1 draw with France. What historical significance did his goal have?

5. When Wolves won the FA Cup in 1960, they needed a replay to get past the third round, winning 4-2 at Molineux after a 2-2 draw on a northern ground. Flowers scored in both games against which opponents?

6. Between 1958 and 1963, he played in 40 consecutive internationals for England, which places him second in the award for most consecutive England games. Who is the only player ahead of him?

7. A goal that probably gave him a lot of pleasure was the only one of the league game at Molineux on 11 April 1955, which kept Wolves in the title race. It came against one of their traditional rivals. Which one?

8. Why did Ron Flowers not get much sleep on the night of 29 July 1966?

9. His last league goal for Wolves in 1965 was his contribution to an 8-2 hammering of which club who often fell victim to the Wolves attack in that era?

10. Which club did he play 61 league games for at the end of his career?

QUIZ No. 30

LEGENDS No. 5 - SIR JACK HAYWARD

1. Sir Jack Hayward bought the club for £2.1 million in which year?

2. For how many years did he own and control the ups and downs of Wolverhampton Wanderers?

3. What was the nominal sum involved when he sold the club to Steve Morgan and what strings were attached to the deal?

4. What role did he have at the club after his period of ownership had ended?

5. Cricket was another sport he loved. Which county was he a life member of, and which event did he sponsor in 1973 in that sport?

6. Which Party leader did he lend financial and other support to in the October 1974 General Election?

7. Complete this quote from Sir Jack in 2003: 'Every time we lose I feel like running a ... ' You need six more words.

8. Three other members of his family have served on the board at Molineux, two of them as chairman. Who are the three?

9. Which stand at Molineux was renamed 'The Sir Jack Hayward Stand' after his death in 2015?

10. The training complex at Compton was also named after him, as was a street near the ground that was retitled 'Jack Hayward Way' in celebration of his birthday in 2003. What was the street formerly called?

QUIZ No. 31

LEGENDS No. 6 - KENNY HIBBITT

1. Kenny Hibbitt scored just two goals in 32 league games in season 1970/71. The strange thing was that both of them were against the same London club, one at home and one away. His goal in the away game was his first goal for Wolves. Who were they playing?

2. On 2 December 1970, he received his only representative honour as a substitute in an England under-23s game. Which British country was it against?

3. His goalscoring improved significantly around the mid-1970s when he was top scorer in the league for Wolves in 1974/75 and again in 1976/77. He scored the same total in each of those seasons. What was it?

4. In his time at Molineux, he scored in one FA Cup semi-final. On what ground, in which year and against which team?

5. The game itself didn't linger long in the memory. The date was 17 February 1973 and Wolves and Newcastle drew 1-1 at Molineux. Why was it probably for him the most memorable game he played in?

6. After scoring one of the goals that won the League Cup for Wolves in the 1974 final, he played a big part in getting them to Wembley again for the 1980 final, scoring four of the 15 goals Wolves got to win it. Those four goals made him Wolves' top goalscorer in the competition that season. True or false?

7. He got his first brace of goals against this club from the North West on 25 March 1972 in a 2-2 away draw, and ended up scoring more goals against them than any other club. Who were they?

8. He scored four times for Wolves in a match just once, in a 4-2 home league win on 24 August 1974. Who were they playing?

9. Kenny scored a hat-trick in a 5-2 win at Molineux on 31 March 1975 against which club?

10. At the end of a phenomenal Wolves career that saw him play nearly 600 games in all competitions and break the appearance record for the club in the League Cup, he started over 50 games for a club from the south west of the country. Which one?

QUIZ No. 32

LEGENDS No. 7 - BILLY WRIGHT

1. Billy started out as an inside-forward at the end of the war. On which three London grounds did he score for Wolves in the Football League South in the 1945/46 season?

2. In that same competition in the same season he scored the only hat-trick of his career on 23 February 1946 in a 4-0 home win against which Midlands club?

3. Manager Ted Vizard moved Billy into the defence and it was a decision that paid dividends for the rest of his career. He captained Wolves when they won the FA Cup at Wembley in 1949. What number was on the back of his shirt on that day?

4. Which club from London did Billy Wright score against the most times in his career?

5. Billy, jointly with Bobby Moore, holds the record for captaining England the most times. How many?

6. In the 1957/58 season, Billy scored both home and away against clubs that share the same first letter of their name and their shirt colour and design. Who were the two clubs?

7. Billy was the first man to reach 100 caps for England. Who were their opponents at Wembley in April 1959 when he attained that milestone in a 1-0 win?

8. When Billy got married, although it was not quite the same media circus as that surrounding the Beckham nuptials some 40 years later, it did cause quite a stir because he married one of a trio of sisters who were a well-known singing group. Who became his wife?

9. Which club did he manage after his retirement?

10. Between October 1951 and May 1959, how many consecutive games did Billy Wright play for England?

QUIZ No. 33

MANAGERS - PART 1

1. Which Wolves manager played in the Borussia Dortmund side that beat Juventus to win the Champions League in 1997?

2. Who are the only two Wolves managers to score in a League Cup Final or replay during their playing careers? If it helps, it was for the same club.

3. Which Wolves manager this century has had the longest spell in the job?

4. Who took over when that man was sacked in 2012 but was unable to change things for the better?

5. Stale Solbakken was next in line, but lasted less than a year. Which country did he come from?

6. Which manager won both the Division Four and Division Three titles back-to-back in the 1980s with Wolves?

7. Who is the only Wolves manager to have the first letter of his first name and surname in the last four letters of the alphabet?

8. Who is the only man to have two spells of management at Wolves? They came between 1968 and 1976, and then again briefly in 1985.

9. Which legendary figure whose name sounds like a Cambridgeshire hospital ran Wolves from 1885 to 1922?

10. Who was the only man to play for Wolves in the 1960s and manage them in the 1980s?

QUIZ No. 34

MANAGERS – PART 2

1. Which Wolves manager played for Watford in the 1984 FA Cup Final against Everton?

2. Which man who led the club between 1927 and 1944 used a military title?

3. Which two Wolves managers have also managed England?

4. Which two Wolves managers played on opposite sides in the 1954 FA Cup Final between West Bromwich Albion and Preston North End?

5. Wolves have been managed by two 'Sammys' whose surnames also begin with the same letter. Who are they?

6. Who is the only man to manage Wolves in both the 1970s and 1980s?

7. In what position did Wolves manager Nuno Spirito Santo play during his footballing career?

8. Who is the only man to manage Wolves in both the 20th and the 21st centuries?

9. An easy one! Who is the only manager to win the league with Wolves?

10. Which Wolves manager was a member of the Aberdeen side that won the 1983 European Cup Winners' Cup Final against Real Madrid?

QUIZ No. 35

MOLINEUX

1. Wolves played at three grounds before their final move to Molineux. Windmill Field was the first from 1877. In 1879 they upped sticks to John Harper's Field. Where did they play between 1881 and 1889 when Molineux became their home?

2. 7 September 1889 saw Molineux's first league game in front of 4,000 spectators with the home side winning 2-0. Who were their first visitors?

3. 17,500 people watched Derby County play Sheffield United at Molineux in 1902. What were they watching?

4. The attendance record for the ground was set on 11 February 1939 in a fifth-round FA Cup tie. The 61,315 present saw Wolves beat which team on their way to Wembley?

5. Which stand opened in 1932, was declared unsafe in 1975 and knocked down in 1978?

6. Which one of Scotland, Wales and Ireland has not faced England in an international at Molineux?

7. Molineux was used for the first time as a venue for an England international against foreign opposition in 1956 when which Scandinavian country came over to play England?

8. In that match, a Manchester United player scored the only hat-trick scored on the ground in an international. Sadly, he was to lose his life two years later in the Munich air crash. Who was he?

9. The Waterloo Road Stand was the victim of arson attacks in 1992, but was transformed under a new name the following year. What was it renamed?

10. The John Ireland Stand was renamed in 2003. What was its new name?

QUIZ No. 36

MULTIPLE CHOICE - PART 1

1. Which club, on 13 September 1966, became Wolves' first ever opponents in the League Cup?
   (a) Mansfield Town (b) Middlesbrough (c) Millwall
   (d) Manchester City

2. When Geoff Palmer, who played over 400 times for Wolves, finally called it a day in 1987, what occupation was he employed in?
   (a) Fireman, (b) Social Worker (c) Teacher (d) Policeman

3. Peter Knowles cut short a very promising career at Wolves when he joined which religious group in 1969?
   (a) The Mormons (b) The Jehovah's Witnesses
   (c) The Moonies (d) The children of God

4. When popular centre-forward Don Goodman left Wolves in 1998, he joined which club?
   (a) Hamilton Academical (b) Hednesford Town
   (c) Hiroshima Antlers (d) Houston Hyundai

5. Wolves have scored over 100 league goals in four consecutive seasons, but came close to conceding 100 in 1905/06 when they let in how many?
   (a) 96 (b) 97 (c) 98 (d) 99

6. Which Wolves player became England's first substitute in a full international when he replaced Jackie Milburn of Newcastle United against Belgium in May 1950?
   (a) Jesse Pye (b) Jimmy Mullen (c) Johnny Hancocks
   (d) Dennis Wilshaw

7. In the first league season of 1888/89, 12 teams entered the competition. Where did Wolves finish?
   (a) third (b) 12th (c) fifth (d) first

8. Bert Williams will always be the 'King of Keepers' at Molineux, but Wolves had another keeper called Williams who played 13 games for the club between 1963 and 1969. What was his first name?
   (a) Eric (b) Eddie (c) Ernie (d) Evan

9. Wolves' record win was in a second-round FA Cup tie on 13 November 1886 against, perhaps unsurprisingly, Crosswell's Brewery! What was the score?
   (a) 11-0 (b) 12-0 (c) 13-0 (d) 14-0

10. Which club visited Molineux on the opening day of the season on two occasions in the 1980s?
    (a) Liverpool (b) Luton Town (c) Leeds United (d) Leicester City

MULTIPLE CHOICE - PART 2

1. What was the nickname of Wolves captain and manager Stan Cullis?
   (a) Flipper (b) Kipper (c) Dipper (d) Nipper

2. Which one of these words with a religious theme has never played for Wolves?
   (a) Pope (b) Deacon (c) Parsonage (d) Church

3. Which Wolves player was sent off at Molineux on 2 October 1996 having scored for them against Bolton Wanderers earlier in the game?
   (a) Darren Ferguson (b) Keith Curle (c) Neil Emblen
   (d) Mark Venus

4. Who scored five goals against Wolves on 30 August 1958?
   (a) Bobby Charlton (b) Jimmy Greaves (c) Bobby Smith
   (d) Nat Lofthouse

5. Which of these clubs have Wolves not met in a League Cup semi-final?
   (a) Spurs (b) Norwich City (c) Leicester City (d) Swindon Town

6. Which one of these towns in Somerset has played for Wolves?
   (a) Bridgwater (b) Chard (c) Wells (d) Frome

7. In 1987/88, the year that Wolves got out of the bottom tier of English football, there were four Welsh clubs in that division. Which one was promoted as runner-up to Wolves?
   (a) Newport County (b) Swansea City (c) Wrexham (d) Cardiff City

8. When Wolves reached the FA Cup Final in 1920/21, they became the first club to play in an FA Cup Final on four different grounds. Which one of these venues did they not play on?
   (a) Lillie Bridge (b) Fallowfield (c) Crystal Palace
   (d) Stamford Bridge

9. Wolves are one of seven clubs who have won the FA Cup while playing in the old Second Division. Which one of these has not done so?
   (a) West Brom (b) Sunderland (c) West Ham (d) Portsmouth

10. The largest average attendance at Molineux for a league season was 45,346. In what season?
    (a) 1946/47 (b) 1948/49 (c) 1949/50 (d) 1950/51

QUIZ No. 38

OCCUPATIONAL WOLVES

All the players' names that constitute the answers here are occupations and there are often clues in the way I've asked the question.

1. He was centre-forward in the Wolves side that killed off Everton to win the FA Cup for the first time in 1893.

2. He came from Norwich City in 1989 and eventually moved on to Coventry City in 1994. Between these dates, he served up some fine performances for Wolves in over 200 games in all competitions.

3. Some thought him a bit agricultural, but his scoring record for Wolves was phenomenal. He came to the club in 1956, but didn't get a game until the 1960s. By the time he retired in 1964, he had scored 44 goals in 57 games for Wolves. As a bonus point, which player had that identical record in internationals for England?

4. Two occupations appeared for Wolves in the 1889 FA Cup Final against Preston North End, one being concerned with the making of arrows, while the other was concerned with their use. Who were the two men?

5. Over 100 years ago, Wolves had a Jerry and a Jimmy, but in the 1950s it was Bobby who came to the fore in building the club. What surname did they share?

6. Who served Wolves from 1982 to 1985, when he moved on to Hereford United?

7. It sounds like it might be illegal, but when he turned out for Wolves in the 1949 FA Cup Final against Leicester City, he was the third person in the club's history to have this surname.

8. A member of an elite medieval occupation played for Wolves in the 1889 FA Cup Final against Preston North End. Who was he?

9. Rose to the heights in the footballing world and captained Wolves in the FA Cup Final of 1960, when they beat Blackburn Rovers at Wembley.

10. Wolves did have a player with this surname who played 18 times for the club between 1919 and 1921, but they are perhaps more likely to remember the name as belonging to the Bournemouth left-winger who cut Wolves down to size by scoring the winner at Molineux in the FA Cup fourth round of 1956/57. It was like a knife to the heart for Wolves because the Third Division South club's scorer also broke the goalpost when he got that vital goal. What surname is involved here?

QUIZ No. 39

OPENING DAY

1. Who are the only club to play Wolves at Molineux on the opening day of successive seasons? It happened in the 1912/13 and 1913/14 seasons.

2. Wolves' first opening day hat-trick came at Molineux on 28 August 1937. Gordon Clayton was responsible for it. Which Lancastrians were beaten 3-1?

3. Wolves made a tremendous start to the first season after World War Two. On 31 August 1946, helped by a Jesse Pye hat-trick, they won 6-1 at Molineux against which London club?

4. 43,000 Wolves fans went home happy from the opening day's game of the 1956/57 season after Manchester City were sent packing from Molineux with a 5-1 defeat. Who scored four of the five goals?

5. A Bobby Mason hat-trick on the opening day of the 1958/59 season contributed to a 5-1 win over which Midlands club at Molineux?

6. What a start Wolves made to the 1962/63 season when Manchester City, not for the first time, were on the wrong end of a high-scoring game. Who got four of Wolves' goals in their 8-1 win?

7. On which ground did Wolves play their first league game of the 2020/21 season?

8. Steve Bull got his name on the goalscorers' sheet on seven opening games, but scored a hat-trick just once, on 17 August 1996 in a 3-1 away win. Where?

9. Who came off the bench to equalise for Wolves at Plymouth Argyle in the 2-2 draw that started their 2008/09 season?

10. Whose two goals were crucial to Wolves' 2-0 win at Carrow Road against Norwich City on 9 August 1997 in the game that opened that season?

QUIZ No. 40

OTHER COMPETITIONS

1. Wolves and West Bromwich Albion produced an exciting encounter in the Charity Shield on 29 September 1955 which was played later than usual that year. What was the score?

2. Which competition did Wolves win in the 1970/71 season by overcoming Dundee United, Morton, Derry City and Hearts?

3. They played each team home and away over the season in that tournament. What was unusual about Wolves' results?

4. In 1985/86 and 1986/87, which competition did Wolves enter, their most thrilling game in those years being a 4-3 home win over Bournemouth on 16 December 1986?

5. In 1987/88, Wolves won the Sherpa Van Trophy after accounting for Swansea, Bristol City, Brentford, Peterborough, Torquay and Notts County to reach the final at Wembley on 29 May 1988. Who did they meet in that final and what was the score?

6. Who scored in all seven games that got Wolves to the final, but drew a blank on that day itself?

7. Wolves defended the Sherpa Van Trophy all the way to a two-leg final the following season. Who did they disappointingly lose to 2-0 at Molineux after winning the away leg 2-1?

8. In three seasons starting in 1989/90, Wolves played Sheffield United, Leicester City, Leeds United and Grimsby Town in which competition?

9. In 1994/95, which tournament pitched Wolves against Lecce, Ascoli, Venezia and Atalanta?

10. In the July before the start of the 1972/73 season, Wolves lost 2-0 at Bristol Rovers in front of 12,489 fans in the first round of which competition?

QUIZ No. 41

PLAY-OFFS AND PENALTY SHOOT-OUTS

1. The strangest play-off Wolves have been involved in came in 1973 when the FA decided, for reasons best known to themselves, that after the FA Cup Final between Sunderland and Leeds United, a match should be played between the losing semi-finalists to decide third place. It took place on 18 August, Wolves running out 3-1 winners against which club? It brings to mind the match played for third place in the World Cup, one of life's absurdities.

2. Wolves first involvement with the play-offs came in the 1986/87 season. They were trying to get out of Division Four and, after seeing off Colchester United, they found which club a bridge too far, going down 3-0 on aggregate?

3. Which Lancastrians beat Wolves in the Division One play-off semi-final 3-2 on aggregate in 1994/95?

4. Which London club denied Wolves the chance of a place in the Premier League in the 1996/97 season despite a 2-1 second-leg Molineux win in the play-off semi-final?

5. Wolves were eliminated at the semi-final stage of the First Division play-offs in 2001/02 by 3-2 on aggregate. Who beat them?

6. The following season produced a memorable outcome for supporters when Wolves reached the Premier League at the Millennium Stadium in the play-off final, winning 3-0 on the day. Who did they beat and which three players found the net for them?

7. Which club knocked Wolves out of the League Cup on penalties in the 2018/19 season?

8. Which Yorkshire club's FA Cup ties against Wolves in 1994/95 and again in 1999/2000 both went to penalties?

9. Which club knocked Wolves out of the 2004/05 League Cup on penalties?

10. Wolves went out of the same competition in the same way two years later as well. Who beat them on this occasion?

QUIZ No. 42

POLITICAL WOLVES

All these players' surnames have been either Presidents of the United States or British Prime Ministers.

1. Played 16 games in goal for Wolves in 1986. In that same season he ended up playing in all four divisions of the Football League, constituting a new record. Who was he?

2. He arrived from Ipswich Town in 1972, playing over 50 times for Wolves in all competitions before joining Hereford United in 1976. Who was he?

3. He played 27 times in the league between 1934 and 1936, scoring six goals before a move to Coventry City. He shares his full name with a Quentin Tarantino film from 1997. Who was he?

4. He played over 100 competitive games for Wolves covering nine different positions after signing for them in 1963. He left to join Bristol City in 1971. Who was he?

5. This midfielder came from Hearts in 2001, playing over 160 times for Wolves before moving to Coventry City in 2006. Who was he?

6. This left-sided player came to the club in 2001. After 160 games he left for Crystal Palace in 2006. Who was he?

7. This midfielder was loaned to Wolves by Aston Villa in 1983 and made ten appearances before returning to his parent club. Who was he?

8. This goalkeeper, who came to Molineux from Huddersfield Town in 1973, played over 100 games for Wolves, including winning a League Cup winner's medal before, in 1979, returning to Yorkshire with Barnsley. Who was he?

9. This defender played just three times on loan at Wolves in 1985 in a career that took in Luton Town, West Brom and Fulham. Who was he?

10. This central-defender, who came to the club in 2011 from Birmingham City, turned out more than 60 times for Wolves before, in 2015, after loan periods at Sheffield Wednesday and West Ham United, he joined Charlton Athletic. Who was he?

QUIZ No. 43

QUOTES

1. Which former Wolves captain, when manager of promotion contenders Charlton Athletic in 1981, said, 'We're half-way round the Grand National course with many hurdles to clear, so let's make sure we all keep our feet firmly on the ground'?

2. Which Wolves manager said of Steve Bull, 'People say his first touch isn't good, but he usually scores with his second'?

3. Who said, on taking the job of Wolves manager, 'I've had more clubs than Jack Nicklaus'?

4. Which Wolves striker said in 2004, 'The day I get my bearings in front of goal, people won't be talking about Thierry Henry any more'?

5. Which player, who eventually became Wolves manager, said, 'After I joined Celtic, I was walking down a street in Glasgow when someone shouted "Fenian bastard". I had to look it up, Fenian that is'?

6. Which Wolves manager said, after a rather traumatic game against Bolton Wanderers, 'I've no qualms about playing in Uriah Rennie's charity golf event, although I might be tempted to wrap my five iron round his neck'?

7. To which Wolves player did Jock Stein say, during a meal with the Scotland team, 'You're from Drumchapel, laddie. What do you know about prawn cocktails? You'll have soup like the rest of us'?

8. Which Wolves player, with great humility, said, 'After Bobby Moore, I'm probably the greatest player to come out of West Ham. Which is to their credit'?

9. Who said, before Wolves FA Cup semi-final with Arsenal in 1998, 'I only hope Tony Adams plays because he's the only name I know. All these Viallis, Vieiras and Viagras. I prefer old fashioned names like Cullis and Wright'?

10. 'If we had got him for £500,000 and played him in our reserves for a couple of seasons, we might have been interested.' Which manager's comments on the transfer of Robbie Keane from Wolves to Coventry City would have raised a few hackles at Molineux?

QUIZ No. 44

SUBLIME SCORES

1. Which club did Wolves beat 7-2 and 7-3 in league games at Molineux in the 1950s?

2. In the 1990s, which away ground did Wolves win on by scores of 6-1 and 5-1?

3. Wolves scored six goals in a game only three times in the whole of the 1980s, but they all came in the same season of 1988/89, two of them in successive home games at Molineux. Which clubs were beaten 6-0, 6-1 and 6-2?

4. In the 1970s, Wolves scored seven times in a game just once in the whole decade. The venue was Molineux and the date was 15 March 1975. Which club returned to London feeling like Julius Caesar?

5. Between 1956 and 1958, one southern club dreaded playing Wolves. In that time, in league and cup games, they lost 6-0, 5-1, 5-3 and 7-0. Who were they?

6. Between 1948 and 1951, which Yorkshire club were hammered 7-1 by Wolves on no less than three occasions, twice at Molineux and once on their own ground?

7. Which newly promoted London club got slaughtered 9-0 at Molineux on 16 September 1959?

8. Until Leicester City's 9-0 win at Southampton in 2019, the biggest away win in the top flight had been Wolves' victory by 9-1 on whose ground on 3 September 1955?

9. A close rival to Wolves in the 1950s and early 1960s, they were beaten 6-1 at Molineux on 30 March 1960 and 7-2 on 13 April 1963 on the same ground. Who were they?

10. Just before World War Two, Wolves got two sevens against this club. Firstly, they beat them 7-2 at Molineux in February 1937 and then by 7-0 on the same pitch in the same month in 1939. Who were they?

QUIZ No. 45

TRANSFERS - 1888-1939

1. A great goalscorer for Wolves, finding the net over 70 times for the club, George Hedley joined in 1906 from a southern non-league club. Earlier, in 1898, Harry Wood, who scored over 120 goals for Wolves, went the other way, signing for that same southern club. Which one?

2. The oldest man to play in a Wolves shirt, when he turned out against Everton at the age of 41 after a transfer from Glossop in 1905, only managed seven goals for the club. Who was he?

3. Perhaps the most contentious transfer of this period saw a Welshman move to Arsenal after 57 goals in 177 games in a Wolves shirt. The £14,000 fee was a British record, but with the war as a major factor Wolves ended up having the better of the deal. Who was the talented player?

4. Which popular forward came from Crewe Alexandra in 1907 and moved to Manchester United 13 years later after a highly successful Wolves career that saw him score 49 goals in 345 games for the club?

5. He came to Molineux in December 1923 from Swindon Town for £1,000, and moved on to Sheffield United for four times that amount in 1928. Between those dates, he scored 104 goals in 144 games in the league for Wolves. Who was he?

6. Which goalkeeper came to the club from Accrington in March 1929 for £400 before a move to Fulham in 1932 after playing 138 games for the Wanderers? He was called the 'bird catcher' because of his ability plucking crosses from the air!

7. Billy Hartill scored 162 goals for Wolves in 221 league games between 1928 and 1935. A local lad, he moved on to which northern club?

8. Reg Weaver came to Wolves from Newport County in 1927 and chalked up 29 goals in 50 games before trying his luck in the capital in 1929, with which club?

9. Defender Tom Dunn joined Wolves in 1891, coming down from East Stirling. After reaching a total of 88 games in the league he moved to which club in Lancashire in 1896?

10. One of the finest goalkeepers in the club's history, he played over 300 times for the Wanderers between spells at Burslem Port Vale and Bradford Park Avenue. In his time at Wolves between 1896 and 1907, he gained five England caps. Who was he?

TRANSFERS - 1945-59

1. Which club immediately after the war provided Wolves with Bert Williams and Johnny Hancocks, two players who between them played over 750 games for Wolverhampton Wanderers?

2. Between 1956 and 1957, Wolves sold goalkeeper Noel Dwyer to this London club and bought dashing winger Harry Hooper from them. Which club?

3. Between 1951 and 1952, Brentford supplied Wolves with two players who went on to make over 830 appearances for the club, one of them returning there late in his career. Who were these two purchases?

4. Which prolific goalscorer came from Notts County in 1946 and left for Luton Town in 1952 after finding the net 95 times for the Molineux club?

5. Which forward came through junior football in 1952 before scoring 26 goals in 78 league games for Wolves, finally leaving for Nottingham Forest in 1959?

6. He came to Wolves from New Brighton before the war and scored over 100 goals in 128 league games before being allowed to move to Blackburn Rovers in 1948. What a career he might have had but for the war! At Ewood Park, he carried on as before, grabbing 37 goals in 63 games for Rovers. Who was he?

7. Tom Galley turned out for the club over 200 times both sides of World War Two and scored in the 1939 FA Cup semi-final against the team he ended up leaving Wolves for in 1947. Who were that team?

8. Sammy Smyth and Dennis Wilshaw scored over 150 goals between them for Wolves. Eventually, they joined the same club. Which one?

9. After 35 goals in 52 games for Wolves, Dickie Dorsett joined which Midlands club in 1947?

10. Scottish inside-forward Jimmy Dunne played 123 league games for Wolves, scoring 33 times before finishing his career between 1952 and 1954 at which Midlands club?

QUIZ No. 47

TRANSFERS – THE 1960s

1. One of the best pieces of business in the history of the club came when Wolves persuaded Kenny Hibbitt to leave this Yorkshire club in 1968. He probably didn't need much persuading as his original club left the league after the 1969/70 season. Who were they?

2. In 1965 John Holsgrove joined Wolves from this club, going on to play over 200 times for Wolves in all competitions. A year or so later Wolves sold Bobby Woodruff to the same side that Holsgrove had come from. Who were they?

3. Which centre-forward came to Wolves from Ipswich Town in 1963, scored 39 goals from 57 league outings for the club, and then went on to West Brom in 1965 where he was less successful?

4. Another centre-forward, Frank Wignall, came to Wolves from a Midlands club in 1967, scored 15 times in 32 games, then left in 1968 for another Midlands club. These two clubs don't care for each other too much! Who are they?

5. After coming through the ranks and playing just 22 times for Wolves, Liverpool took such a fancy to him that they made him Britain's most expensive teenager when paying Wolves £100,000 for his services in September 1968. Who was he?

6. Once a Wanderer, always a Wanderer! Which Wolves player, who made over 240 appearances for the club in all competitions, joined Bolton Wanderers in 1967 and got into three figures there as well?

7. After being instrumental in Liverpool's rise from the Second Division in 1961/62, which creative player come to Molineux in 1964 before joining Southampton the following year?

8. Which two members of Wolves' FA Cup-winning side of 1960 joined Manchester City, one of them in 1963 and the other in the next year?

9. He joined Wolves in 1966 after spells at Southampton and Crystal Palace, playing in 40 league games before going west to Plymouth Argyle in 1968. He had started at the Albion and the nation had witnessed his ball juggling skills live on television when he was a teenager. Who was he?

10. Gerry Harris had given Wolves excellent service at full-back since 1953, playing in over 270 games for the club. Which club, also in the Midlands, did he join in the mid-1960s?

QUIZ No. 48

TRANSFERS – THE 1970s

1. Which left winger, who had played for England while with Huddersfield Town early in his career, joined Wolves from Leeds United in 1969, played 28 times for the club before exiting to Birmingham City on loan and then joining Rotherham United in 1972?

2. A great player for the Wolves, Mike Bailey had come from Charlton Athletic in 1965 and took part in over 350 league games for Wolves before moving to America to play for which club?

3. Which forward signed for Wolves from Norwich City in 1969 and left for Oxford United in 1972 after scoring 40 times in 82 league appearances for the Molineux men?

4. Which bustling centre-forward had two spells at Wolves, the first at the start of the decade and the second half way through it? He scored over 30 goals in the 70-plus games he played for the Wanderers, eventually joining Bristol Rovers in 1977.

5. He became a legend at a club not a million miles from Molineux at the start of the next decade for scoring the most important goal in the club's history. After playing just once for Barrow he came to Wolves in 1973, played for the club 17 times and left for Birmingham City in 1975. Who was he?

6. This central defender started out at Wolves in 1977 before moving to QPR in 1979. He returned to Molineux for a solitary game in the next decade. Who was he?

7. More well known at Burnley and QPR, this winger came to Wolves from Everton in 1979 and started ten league games for the club before trying his luck in Canada at the start of the next decade. Who was he?

8. Reliable defender Dave Woodfield left Wolves in 1971 after 250 games in the league for them, joining another club beginning with a 'W'. Which one?

9. After more than 100 games for Hull City he came to Wolves in 1978, turning out more than 150 times for them. In the following decade he joined Sunderland. Who was this dependable defender?

10. Emlyn Hughes was past his best when he came from Liverpool in 1979, but was an inspiration in the Wolves side that lifted the League Cup trophy the following year. Which club did he leave Wolves for a year later?

QUIZ No. 49

TRANSFERS – THE 1980s

1. Which midfielder, whose initials suggest he might be useful if your car broke down, joined Wolves after playing for Barnsley and a brief spell in Hong Kong and left for Blackburn Rovers in 1985 after 58 games for Wolves?

2. Which Scot played 64 league games for Wolves after arriving from Celtic in 1983, before departing north again to Dundee in 1985?

3. Which popular forward came to the club from non-league Southport in 1986, scoring over 100 goals before moving on in the next decade to Swindon Town?

4. Which Wolves forward, unlucky enough to sustain a broken leg against Crystal Palace in a fifth-round FA Cup tie in 1979, played 80 games for the club from 1973 until his transfer to Blackburn Rovers in 1981?

5. This forward played more than 170 times for Wolves after coming through junior football. Between 1977 and 1983, he found the net 33 times before trying his luck down the road at Birmingham. He returned to Molineux for one game in the 1990s. Who was he?

6. Which full-back, after eight years at Molineux comprising over 160 games, was transferred to Charlton Athletic in 1985, and subsequently also played for Crystal Palace?

7. After over a decade at Wolves during which he played over 200 matches for the club, he moved on to Sheffield United via Huddersfield Town in the mid-1980s. Who was he?

8. This guy had a complex career pattern having two spells at both Everton and Luton Town. He was at Wolves in 1985, joining from Swedish club Orebero SK. Perhaps the high point of his career came when he scored the winner for Everton in the Merseyside derby in 1978. Who was he?

9. What is the link between the moves away from Molineux in the 1980s of Wolves players John Richards, Paul Bradshaw and Colin Brazier?

10. Which player joined Wolves from Derby County in 1985 and made nearly 200 appearances for the club before moving south to Reading in 1990?

QUIZ No. 50

TRANSFERS - THE 1990s

1. This Birmingham-born midfielder started out at the Villa before moving to Molineux in 1991. He started 128 league games for Wolves before his transfer to Doncaster Rovers in 1996. Who was he?

2. Coming the other way from Doncaster to Wolverhampton in 1992 was another midfielder who featured in over 100 league matches for Wolves before a move to Preston North End in 1996. Who was he?

3. This whole-hearted central defender came to the club from Bradford City in 1992. After appearing in just under 100 league games he left for Southampton in the last year of the decade and later enjoyed success at Tottenham Hotspur. Who was he?

4. Towards the end of the 1990s, Wolves recruited two players from German football, one from Werder Bremen and one from Fortuna Dusseldorf. One of them made only a handful of appearances before returning to Germany, but the other was more successful. Who were the two men?

5. This midfielder won nine England caps at Crystal Palace before a move to Wolves in 1993. He left for Nottingham Forest in 1997, but not before chalking up just over 50 games for the Molineux club. Who was he?

6. Which lively forward came to Wolves in 1993 from Newcastle United and wore the black and old gold just over 100 times before a return to the North East with Sunderland in 1995?

7. Wolves got a real bargain when West Brom let this versatile player go in 1986. Over 450 games and 45 goals later, he left for Tranmere Rovers in 1994. Who was he?

8. A Yorkshire-born full-back, his Wolves career in the mid-1990s was sandwiched between spells at Sheffield Wednesday and Barnsley, but he turned out for Wolves on over 80 occasions. Who was he?

9. This winger started out at Aston Villa before appearing in the North East with Middlesbrough and Darlington. He came to Wolves in 1991, played over 70 times for them and then joined Port Vale in 1994. Who was he?

10. Darlington also figured in this man's career. He joined them from Wolves in 1993 after playing over 70 times since coming to the Midlands from Sheffield Wednesday in 1991. Who was he?

QUIZ No. 51

TRANSFERS - THE 2000s

1. In this decade Wolves often seemed to go to Sunderland to purchase players. How many such players can you name? If you get seven you are some fan with a memory to match!

2. Michael Gray was also someone who played at Sunderland, but it wasn't from that club that he joined Wolves in 2007. Who sold him?

3. Paul Ince was past his best when he arrived at Molineux but he could still be an inspirational leader. From which club did Wolves obtain his signature in 2002?

4. When Wolves won the Championship in 2008/09 local lad Karl Henry was on the field in all but three of their 46 matches. Which club had earlier sold him to Wolves?

5. From which London club did Wolves buy Shaun Newton in 2001?

6. Wolves defender Mark Edworthy was transferred from which club in 2002?

7. Which centre-forward proved a good buy when he was brought in from Glasgow Rangers in 2001?

8. Which defender arrived from French club Marseilles in 2009?

9. Kevin Cooper in 2002 and Darren Ward in 2007 both came to Molineux from the capital. Which two clubs sold them to Wolves?

10. Having already established that Wolves did well with a player from Rangers, in the middle of the decade Wolves tried their luck with two midfielders from Celtic. Who were they?

QUIZ No. 52

TRANSFERS - THE 2010s

They weren't called Wanderers for nothing in this decade! Wolves had started like many other clubs to look further afield, signing more foreign players than had previously been the case. Can you recall the clubs that Wolves signed the following players from?

1. Rui Patricio

2. Ruben Neves

3. Leander Dendoncker

4. Jonny

5. Ruben Vinagre

6. Raul Jimenez

7. Romain Saiss

8. Bjorn Sigurdarson

9. Rajiv Van La Parra

10. Michal Zyro

QUIZ No. 53

TRUE OR FALSE - PART 1

1. Wolves have spent just one season at the fourth level of English football. True or false?

2. Andy Gray scored more than twice as many goals in total for Wolves as he did for Everton. True or false?

3. Among clubs who have lost an FA Cup Final at Wembley before World War Two, Wolves were the first one to win one after the war. True or false?

4. No other club in the decade between 2010/11 and 2019/20 bettered Wolves' points total of 99 in winning the championship of 2017/18? True or false?

5. Wolves have finished runners-up in the top flight on five occasions, never being more than four points off the champions. True or false?

6. Wolves won 5-0 at Elm Park against Reading in the FA Cup third round in 1910. True or false?

7. From the outset of the Football League in 1888/89, Wolves won all their first five games against Burnley with an aggregate score of 22 goals against four. True or false?

8. Wolves' 10-1 win over Leicester City on 15 April 1938 still stands as their biggest-ever league win. True or false?

9. Wolves have played in an FA Cup Final as a Second Division club and also played against a Second Division club in an FA Cup Final. True or false?

10. In 1976/77, both the Football Writers' 'Player of the Year' and the PFA award went to players who later joined Wolves. True or false?

QUIZ No. 54

TRUE OR FALSE - PART 2

1. Wolves have played an FA Cup semi-final at both Anfield and Goodison Park. True or false?

2. No Wolves player in the team that beat Blackburn Rovers to win the 1960 FA Cup Final had previously played in an FA Cup Final. True or false?

3. Jesse Pye, in 1949, has been the only player with a surname of three letters to score in a post-war FA Cup Final. True or false?

4. Wolves came into being due to an amalgamation of a football club and a rugby club. True or false?

5. Wolves had no player in the 20th century whose surname began with a 'Q'. True or false?

6. Wolves have played more FA Cup finals at Wembley than in all other venues put together. True or false?

7. Blackburn Rovers are the only club that Wolves have both won and lost an FA Cup semi-final against. True or false?

8. Jimmy Utterson, between 1934 and 1936, was the only player in the 20th century to play for Wolves with a surname beginning with a 'U'. True or false?

9. Wolves have won the League Cup more times than West Brom, the same number of times as Birmingham City, but fewer times than Leicester City. True or false?

10. Wolves have won exactly half of all the FA Cup finals they have contested. True or false?

QUIZ No. 55

TRUE OR FALSE - PART 3

1. Wolves are the only club who play in black and gold to win the League Cup. True or false?

2. Wolves provided England with their entire half-back line of right-half, centre-half and left-half for four consecutive internationals in 1958. True or false?

3. Peter Zelem became the first player whose surname began with the last letter of the alphabet to score for Wolves when he got their first goal of the season at home to Cambridge United on 23 August 1986, a goal that turned out to be his only goal for the club. True or false?

4. Blackburn Rovers are the only club to play in exactly the same number of FA Cup finals as Wolves. True or false?

5. The only time in the 1990s that Molineux witnessed Wolves score six goals in a league game was on 31 March 1992 when they beat Newcastle United 6-2. True or false?

6. Wolves were the only club to win the League Cup in both the 1970s and the 1980s. True or false?

7. Only Dickie Baugh Senior played in all the three FA Cup finals Wolves contested in the 19th century. True or false?

8. Wolves have won the League Cup twice as many times as West Brom. True or false?

9. Stan Fazackerley had a big impact in an FA Cup replay at Molineux on 7 February 1924. He scored the winning goal and then became the first Wolves player to be sent off in an FA Cup tie. True or false?

10. Michal Zyro became the first Wolves player of the current century whose surname begins with a 'Z' when he turned out for them in the 2015/16 season. True or false?

QUIZ No. 56

UNDER THE MOLINEUX LIGHTS

The 1950s were synonymous with the swashbuckling adventures of Wolverhampton Wanderers under their Molineux floodlights where they took on clubs from across the world in 'friendlies' that never looked like they were. Look on the internet to see the intensity! It is hard today to convey just how fascinated the country was by these games, but they were very big news at the time.

1. 'The team I liked best as a boy was Wolves. They were the most glamorous club of the day. They got floodlights and they played Moscow Dynamo.' Which player who went on to be quite useful with another club was talking here about his childhood? A clue is in one of the words he used.

2. The floodlights of which iconic American sports arena were the blueprint for Wolves' floodlights?

3. Wolves, with the second half live on black-and-white television, beat Moscow Dynamo 2-1 on 9 November 1955 at Molineux. Which legendary goalkeeper played for Dynamo that night?

4. As if warming up for their encounter with the two Moscow clubs and the Hungarian champions Honved, Wolves beat an Argentinian side 3-1 in March 1954 and followed this up with a 10-0 autumn hammering of an Israeli club. Who were their two opponents?

5. By what score did Wolves beat Moscow Spartak in November 1954?

6. Which legendary figure captained Honved when they lost 3-2 to Wolves in December 1954?

7. In that game, Wolves trailed 2-0 at half time to the Hungarians. A Wilshaw penalty restored some hope after the interval, before two late goals sent the crowd wild. Which player scored them?

8. It is highly likely that the cup tie atmosphere of these pioneering matches cost Wolves the title in that 1954/55 season when they won just three of their last 11 league games, finishing second and just four points behind which club?

9. It was after the Honved game that the hyperbole really arrived, because in beating the Hungarian champions Wolves had avenged the famous 6-3 Wembley international defeat. Wolves were seen to have put English football back on top, a view that proved to be slightly premature. Bob Ferrier proclaimed, 'Wolves can rightly claim themselves club champions of the world.' Which daily newspaper was he writing for?

10. To celebrate the 50th anniversary of the Honved game, players who were still with us paraded at half time at Molineux in a match in December 2004 that coincided with the first game in charge for which manager?

QUIZ No. 57

VENUES

1. On which ground did Wolves beat Aston Villa 1-0 in the FA Cup semi-final of 1960?

2. At which Birmingham-based venue did Wolves win an FA Cup semi-final against Derby County in 1896?

3. On which northern ground were Wolves successful in two FA Cup semi-finals, the first against Cardiff City in 1921, followed by victory over Grimsby Town in 1939?

4. Besides Wembley, what is the only ground that Wolves have played on in both an FA Cup Final and an FA Cup semi-final?

5. There is only one ground that Wolves have played on in three post-war FA Cup semi-finals. They were in 1949, 1951 and 1981. What is that ground?

6. Which ground, where Wolves played in an FA Cup semi-final replay in 1951, contains the name of another football club in its title?

7. On their way to winning the League Cup in 1980, Wolves drew twice with Grimsby Town in the fifth round, finally progressing by winning the third game 2-0, on which neutral venue?

8. On which London ground did Wolves play Preston North End in the 1889 FA Cup Final?

9. Which ground was rather unfairly chosen as the venue for the FA Cup semi-final replay between Wolves and Spurs in 1981?

10. On which ground did Wolves meet Leeds United in the FA Cup semi-final in 1973?

QUIZ No. 58

WHO AM I?

1. I played in just under 50 games for Wolves near the end of my career in the mid-1990s, signing from Derby County and moving on to Sheffield United. Earlier, I was part of the Blackburn Rovers side that gained promotion to the Premier League in 1991/92, but by far the biggest moment of my career came in the early 1980s when I won the European Cup with another club. But let's not go there! Who am I?

2. I should imagine I am the only Wolves player in their history to join them in one millennium after being substituted in successive seasons in the FA Cup Final when with another club in the previous millennium. Who am I?

3. My career in England thus far is a story of three Augusts. In the first of them in 2015 I joined Aston Villa but we were relegated at the end of the season. The second August in 2016 brought me a move to Middlesbrough and two years later I reached Molineux, scoring my first goal for Wolves in a 1-0 win at West Ham on 1 September. Who am I?

4. I like breaking records. When Wolves sold me, they got more money for me than for any player they had previously sold. I got more caps for my country than any other man, and I scored over three times as many goals for my country as my nearest challenger. Who am I?

5. I was born in Ballymena and came to Molineux from Bournemouth in 1993. In 1997 I moved on to Gillingham after making a dozen appearances for Wolves. I may be unique in being the only golf tournament to play for the club. Who am I?

6. You could say I was well travelled, turning out for a dozen English league clubs, but I didn't stay very long at Wolves after I joined them from Bristol City in 1999. Forty games and 16 goals later I was off again, this time to Leicester. Who am I?

7. I was a local lad who played for Wolves 12 times between 1931 and 1938 when I moved on to Hull City. Thirty years later, I helped out when Wolves had managerial problems, acting as caretaker manager alongside Gerry Summers for a short period. Who am I?

8. I was born in Stafford and broke into the Wolves team in the 2016/17 season. I have made over 50 appearances to date, but am currently out on loan. The first part of my surname is a manufacturer of toothpaste, and the second part is the colour you would hope your teeth would be after using it! Who am I?

9. My brother scored more league goals than anyone in the history of the English game, and I wasn't too far behind. I played for Wolves in the unofficial seasons during World War Two and my two goals in the second leg of the League War Cup Final at Molineux on 30 May 1942 against Sunderland helped deliver that trophy. After the war, two more goals I scored in the 1948 FA Cup Final for Manchester United swung it their way. Who am I?

10. This sounds like a tough one because I only played once for Wolves on my way from Aldershot to Northampton Town in 1961. However, I am remembered in football circles for one thing that looked amusing but actually finished my career. I was playing in goal for Brentford at Colchester United in 1969 when a sheepdog ran onto the pitch and attacked me, causing an injury to my kneecap that didn't heal. Who am I?

QUIZ No. 59

WOLVES AGAINST LANCASHIRE CLUBS

1. Which club, by winning their final game, denied Wolves the first league and cup double of the 20th century in 1959/60? Spurs claimed that honour the following season.

2. Who are the only Lancastrians that Wolves have lost to in an FA Cup Final?

3. Which club knocked Wolves out of the FA Cup on the way to winning it in 1903?

4. Which Lancastrian club had already won the FA Cup five times before Wolves won it for the first time in 1893?

5. In the inaugural league season of 1888/89, which Lancastrian founder member did Wolves draw 4-4 with? They had to wait until 1930 for another 4-4 draw in the league.

6. Which Lancastrians beat Wolves 4-1 in the Charity Shield of 1958?

7. Which team from Lancashire pipped Wolves for the runners-up position on goal average in season 1955/56 when Manchester United were comfortable winners? Under the current system, Wolves would have been second because they scored more goals.

8. Wolves have twice been knocked out of the FA Cup by this Lancastrian club, firstly in the third round of 1929/30, and more recently in the first round after a replay in 2013/14. Who are they?

9. This club appeared in the fifth round of the FA Cup for the first time in their history, when losing 3-1 to Wolves at Molineux in 2003. In the 2004/05 season, they played Wolves again, this time in the League Cup, and lost on this occasion by 4-2. Who are they?

10. Wolves played their last FA Cup tie of the 20th century against this team when they won 1-0 away from home with a Carl Robinson goal on 11 December 1999. Who are they?

QUIZ No. 60

WOLVES AGAINST LONDON CLUBS

1. Which London club were Wolves' first FA Cup opponents of the 20th century when they beat the Wanderers after a replay in January 1900?

2. Which London club lost 4-0 at home and 2-1 away to Wolves in their only season of top-flight football in 1962/63?

3. Who are the only London club to knock Wolves out of the FA Cup on penalties?

4. Who are the only two London clubs that Wolves have finished runners-up to in a top-flight season?

5. Who are the only London club that Wolves have met in an FA Cup Final?

6. The first league season after World War Two in 1946/47 was this London club's only post-war season in the top flight and they were duly relegated at the end of it. However, it didn't stop them from doing the double over high-flying Wolves. Who were they?

7. Which London club did Wolves meet in successive years in the FA Cup in 1993/94 and 1994/95, and then again in 2009/10?

8. When this London club won the FA Cup in 1946, they beat Wolves on the way to the final, and when Wolves won it in 1960, they beat this club on the way to that final. Who are they?

9. Wolves beat this London club in an FA Cup tie in 1897 when they still had the word 'Athletic' after their name. Three quarters of a century later, they met again in an FA Cup tie at Molineux and Wolves won again, although by this time their opponents had dropped the 'Athletic'. Who are they?

10. It started in 1909/10, when Wolves lost an FA Cup tie to them at Molineux by 5-1, and this century hasn't changed much yet as they have knocked Wolves out of the competition again in both 2003/04 and 2015/16. Who are they?

QUIZ No. 61

WOLVES AGAINST MIDLANDS CLUBS
(EXCLUDING WEST BROMWICH ALBION)

1. In the old Second Division of 1966/67, Wolves gained promotion to the top flight as runners-up. During the season, they lost 3-1 both home and away to the eventual champions. Who were they?

2. When Wolves won the league in 1957/58, they would have been very pleased to have beaten which club home and away by 5-1?

3. Which is the only Midlands club that Wolves have met in an FA Cup Final?

4. It took extra time to knock this Midlands club out of the 2010/11 League Cup, but Wolves haven't met them since the 2013/14 season when Wolves were promoted from League One and they were relegated. Who are they?

5. In 2016/17, which Midlands club did Wolves knock out of the FA Cup by 2-0 in the third round on their own patch prior to their exploits at Anfield in round four?

6. Wolves have met just two Midlands clubs in an FA Cup semi-final, the first in 1896 and the second in 1960. On both occasions, Wolves went on to win the cup. Who were the two beaten semi-finalists?

7. Leaving Aston Villa out of the equation, Wolves have won the league title more times than any other Midlands club. True or false?

8. Wolves have met this Midlands club twice in the League Cup, most recently losing at home to them in 1994/95. Wolves would gladly accept that reverse given that an earlier meeting in the same competition had slightly more riding on it and Wolves came out of it in front. Who are they?

9. Which south-east Midlands club did Wolves meet in the League Cup three years in four between the 2011/12 and 2014/15 seasons?

10. Which club from just south west of Nottingham did Wolves beat 4-1 in their very first FA Cup tie on 27 October 1883?

QUIZ No. 62

WOLVES AGAINST YORKSHIRE CLUBS

1. Who are the only Yorkshire club to meet Wolves in an FA Cup Final?

2. On which Yorkshire club's ground did Wolves lose an FA Cup semi-final replay to Newcastle United in 1951?

3. In the 2010/11 season, which Yorkshire side did Wolves knock out of the FA Cup by 5-0 at Molineux after a 2-2 away draw in their first encounter in the third round?

4. Which Yorkshire club, who won the FA Cup in 1911, did Wolves meet for the first time in Division Two on 22 September 1906 when a Jack Roberts hat-trick won the game for Wolves?

5. When Wolves won the Third Division title in 1988/89, which Yorkshire club went up with them as runners-up?

6. In the FA Cup third round of 1968/69, two Derek Dougan goals and one from Frank Wignall secured the 3-1 win over which Yorkshire club?

7. Wolves met this Yorkshire club several times before World War One. They met again in the 1920/21 season when the club had changed the last word of their name. Who had they become?

8. Sheffield United are the only Yorkshire club to have won the FA Cup as many times as Wolves. True or false?

9. This Yorkshire club is the only one to twice knock Wolves out of the League Cup on penalties. It happened in 2002/03 and again in 2008/09. Who are they?

10. 1996/97 was a frustrating season for Wolves, who finished third in Division One but failed to reach the Premier League via the play-offs. Bolton were champions and this Yorkshire club were promoted with them as runners-up. They also provided the most exciting game of the season at Molineux, drawing 3-3 there in November. Who are they?

QUIZ No. 63

WOLVES BARING TEETH (SENDINGS-OFF)

1. On the last day of 1904 in a 2-2 draw at Nottingham Forest, who became the first Wolves player to be sent off in a league game?

2. Which Wolves player, between 1987 and 1997, was sent off six times when in a Wolves shirt?

3. Which Wolves player was sent off for a foul on Bernardo Silva in the away league game with Manchester City on 14 January 2019?

4. It was extremely unusual for a goalkeeper to be sent off in the 1930s, but which Wolves keeper managed it twice in one month in December 1936? It might help if I tell you that he shares his name with a female Sky TV pundit who played for England.

5. In the early 1970s, Wolves had two players dismissed in the away legs of the UEFA Cup. The first came at Academica Coimbra in 1971, and the second at Belenenses in 1973. Who were the two players?

6. As this was the third time they had beaten Wolves in 20 days, in October 1981, he might have been forgiven for 'losing it', but which Wolves player was sent off against Aston Villa in a League Cup tie at Molineux on 27 October 1981?

7. Wolves won the Fair Play League in 1977/78, the only blot on their copybook being the sending off of Bob Hazell in an FA Cup tie on which ground?

8. On which Lancashire ground have Dave Wagstaffe, Dave Woodfield and Kevin Muscat all been sent off playing for Wolves, the first two in the same game?

9. Dave Wagstaffe also holds another record in the 'sent-off stakes' that can't be taken from him. What is it?

10. Which Wolves defender was fined £3,000 for improper conduct after an incident in the tunnel at Middlesbrough in March 2004?

QUIZ No. 64

WOLVES IN EUROPE - 1958-80

1. Wolves entered the European Cup for the first time in 1958/59, but any optimism was soon dashed as they went out 4-3 on aggregate against which German club in the first round?

2. Who scored Wolves' first goal in the European Cup on 12 November 1958 at Molineux, ending up with both of their goals in a 2-2 draw against the answer to question one above?

3. Wolves went out of the 1974/75 UEFA Cup competition in the first round on a 5-4 aggregate score against Porto. Who scored for Wolves in both legs?

4. In the previous season of 1973/74, Wolves looked to have given themselves a hopeless task after a UEFA Cup second-round defeat by 3-0 in the first leg in East Germany. The fans thought so too, with only 14,530 inside Molineux for the second leg. Wolves won 4-1 with goals from Dougan, Hibbitt, Kindon and Munro, but their efforts were in vain because the away-goals rule sank them. Who were their opponents?

5. In 1960/61 Wolves contested a truncated European Cup Winners' Cup tournament, going out against their second opponents over two legs in the semi-final. The team that put Wolves out lost in the final to Fiorentina of Italy. Who were they?

6. In 1971/72 Wolves experienced their best run in Europe when they went all of the way to the UEFA Cup Final before losing over two legs to Spurs. On the way, they knocked out Academica Coimbra, F.C. Den Haag, Carl Zeiss Jena, Juventus and Ferencvaros. Which five countries did these clubs represent?

7. In that season, Wolves won the home leg against F.C. Den Haag by 4-0. What was extremely odd about the goalscorers?

8. Wolves played what proved to be their final match in Europe of the century on 1 October 1980 when they won 1-0 in the second leg of the first round of the UEFA Cup at Molineux. It was not enough to overcome a 3-1 deficit from the away leg. Who knocked them out?

9. Which Wolves player got that last goal in Europe of the 20th century that gave them that 1-0 win?

10. Between 1958 and 1980, Wolves faced 16 clubs in three different European competitions. Five of them have won the European Cup or, as it absurdly became, the Champions League. Who are they?

QUIZ No. 65

WOLVES IN THE EUROPA LEAGUE
- 2019/20

1. Wolves entered the tournament at the second qualifying round stage, defeating which Irish club 6-1 on aggregate?

2. Which Wolves player scored at both ends in the away leg?

3. In the third qualifying round, Wolves beat Pyunik of Armenia by the same score in both legs. What was that score?

4. Which Italian club did Wolves beat 5-3 on aggregate in a play-off to reach the group stage?

5. Which Wolves player scored in the away legs against all three teams which they met in the two qualifying rounds and the play-off?

6. After a disappointing start to the group stage matches when they lost at home to Braga, Wolves put this right with a win in Turkey against Besiktas. Whose 93rd minute winner got the job done?

7. Which Wolves player was sent off in the third group match when Wolves defeated Slovan Bratislava 2-1 on their own ground?

8. After a thrilling 3-3 draw in Braga, Wolves completed their group stage fixtures with a fine 4-0 win over Besiktas at Molineux. In just 12 second-half minutes, a rampant Wolves found the net four times. Diogo Jota scored three of them. Who got the other goal?

9. Wolves eventually reached the quarter-finals by putting out Spanish and Greek opposition in the previous two knock-out rounds. Who were the defeated clubs?

10. It took the eventual winners of the tournament until two minutes from the end of the one-off quarter-final tie to knock Wolves out after their great but exhausting adventure. Who were they?

QUIZ No. 66

WOLVES IN THE FA CUP - 1883-1915

1. In the successive seasons of 1888/89 and 1889/90, Wolves won first-round ties against the same club who played their home games at Charterhouse. They had already won the FA Cup in 1881 and are one of only three clubs whose name begins with 'O' to have done so. Who are they?

2. Whose superb goalscoring record in the FA Cup for Wolves between 1883 and 1890 saw him grab 22 goals in 22 games for the club?

3. In 1884/85 and 1885/86, Wolves won, drew and lost in the FA Cup to a Midlands club whose suffix is the same as one of the clubs Wolves were formed from. Who were they?

4. Which Midlands club that were to become a bitter rival over the years did Wolves meet four times in the FA Cup in 1886/87?

5. Which club did Wolves beat in the FA Cup semi-final in 1888/89 and lose to at the same stage in the following season?

6. Which Midlands club did Wolves encounter on six occasions in the FA Cup between 1896 and 1904?

7. In the 1904/05 season, Wolves exited the competition after two rounds. Their two opponents that year had the same colours but were situated at opposite ends of the country. Who were they?

8. Which Yorkshire club knocked Wolves out of the FA Cup in consecutive seasons in 1913/14 and 1914/15?

9. In which two years in this period did Wolves get their hands on that elusive trophy?

10. Southern clubs started to have a bigger say in the FA Cup in the new century and this was personified by three London clubs eliminating Wolves from the competition in successive seasons in 1908/09, 1909/10 and 1910/11. The middle one has been dealt with elsewhere, but which two clubs from the capital that begin with the same letter were responsible for putting Wolves out on the other two occasions?

QUIZ No. 67

WOLVES IN THE FA CUP - 1919-39

1. In the first cup season back after the war, Wolves were eliminated in the fourth round by a team they gained revenge on in the following season by beating them after a semi-final replay in 1920/21. Who were they?

2. On the road to that FA Cup Final of 1920/21, Wolves played in London once when they won a third-round tie 1-0 against a team that shared their colours with the eventual winners of the trophy. Who did Wolves beat in that third-round match?

3. Besides London, in which city did Wolves play twice during that FA Cup campaign of 1920/21?

4. Which non-league club won at Molineux on 12 January 1929 to put Wolves out of that year's FA Cup tournament? They were subsequently elected into the Football League at the start of the 1931/32 season.

5. Which Welsh club did Wolves put to the sword 9-1 in the third round of the FA Cup in 1930/31?

6. Derby County, Preston North End and West Bromwich Albion all knocked Wolves out of the FA Cup twice between 1919 and 1939, but one club did it three times. Which one?

7. Which club that shares their colours beat Wolves in an FA Cup third-round replay at Molineux in 1924/25, only for Wolves to turn the tables on them by the same score of 1-0 on the same ground in the fifth round two years later?

8. It took three games for the eventual FA Cup winners of 1937 to get past Wolves in the quarter-final. Who were they?

9. Wolves reached the FA Cup Final in 1939 only to go down 4-1 to unfancied Portsmouth. Who scored 11 of the 19 goals that got them to Wembley?

10. Strangely enough, twice during this period when Wolves were knocked out of the FA Cup the score-line and opponents were the same as previous FA Cup finals. The cup exits came in 1922 and 1935, both times against teams that reached the final. What were the results of those previous FA Cup finals that reappeared exactly?

WOLVES IN THE FA CUP - 1945-60

1. Because league football was still regional in 1945/46 the FA Cup was a magnet for fans and was played over two legs for the only time. Wolves' first game saw them beaten 4-2 in Wales by a team that never played league football and which folded in 1969. Wolves were able to hide their blushes by winning the second leg 8-1. Who were this Welsh side?

2. The odds against this happening must be high, but Wolves were drawn in the fourth round of the FA Cup against the same club in 1946/47, 1948/49 and 1949/50. Which Yorkshire club was involved here?

3. Which then current holders of the trophy did Wolves beat after a replay in the FA Cup semi-final of 1948/49 on their way to winning it?

4. On the road to Wembley, that season, Wolves played on two different grounds in the same city. Which city was it?

5. In defence of their trophy in 1949/50, Wolves reached the fifth round before going out in a replay to a club that won the FA Cup for the only time in their history three years later. Who were they?

6. Wolves started off in entertaining fashion in the FA Cup in 1956/57, beating Swansea Town 5-3 in the third round. They were brought down to earth with a bang in the next round when they fell victim to which Division Three South giant-killers?

7. In 1957/58 and 1958/59, Wolves were knocked out of the FA Cup by the same Lancashire club. Who were they?

8. Who were the only two Wolves players in this period to score in both an FA Cup Final and an FA Cup semi-final?

9. Which club from the west of the country were Wolves drawn away to in the third round in the successive seasons 1949/50 and 1950/51?

10. Wolves ended the decade by winning the trophy again in 1959/60. They were fortunate in the final in two ways. Firstly, their first goal just before half time was an own goal, and, secondly, in a world before substitutes, the Blackburn Rovers left-back suffered a broken leg and was stretchered off. Who was responsible for the own goal and who was injured? It may help to say that the latter became a well-known figure.

QUIZ No. 69

WOLVES IN CUP COMPETITIONS – THE 1960s

1. Entering the League Cup later than most clubs, Wolves competed in the last four seasons of the decade, twice going out on grounds in West London, firstly in 1966/67 and then in 1969/70. Which two clubs beat them?

2. FA Cup winners in 1960, Wolves defence of the trophy didn't last long. They were beaten in an away replay in the third round by which Second Division side from Yorkshire?

3. Which London club did Wolves lose to in the FA Cup in 1968/69, but beat in the following season's League Cup?

4. During the course of the decade, six players whose names begin with a 'W' scored goals for Wolves in the FA Cup or the League Cup, or both. Who were they?

5. In two successive seasons, 1964/65 and 1965/66, Wolves had good leads in FA Cup ties at Molineux against the same club. However, the final scores in these matches were 5-3 and 4-2 in favour of the visitors. Who were they?

6. Which local rivals, who had already won on six of the previous seven occasions on which they had been drawn against each other in the FA Cup, added another to their collection when they won 2-1 at Molineux in the fourth round of 1961/62?

7. The only non-league club to play Wolves in the FA Cup in the 1960s did so at Molineux in the third round of 1965/66. They were beaten 5-0 in front of a 30,000 crowd. Who were they?

8. Which Wolves player scored seven goals in seven games in the FA Cup in season 1964/65, including a hat-trick in a second replay with Aston Villa in the fifth round at the Hawthorns?

9. In the final two seasons of the decade in the League Cup, Wolves were drawn to play three teams which represent popular seaside holiday destinations. Who were they?

10. Which Yorkshire club did Wolves knock out of the FA Cup in 1964/65, before being knocked out of the same competition by them three years later?

QUIZ No. 70

WOLVES IN CUP COMPETITIONS – THE 1970s

1. Wolves first League Cup game of the decade saw them exit the competition at the hands of which club, who, at the time, shared their colours?

2. It was a brighter picture in the FA Cup, where their first encounter produced a 5-1 win at Molineux in the third round at the expense of which club?

3. In the 1972/73 season, Wolves reached the FA Cup semi-final, beating Manchester United, Bristol City, Millwall and Coventry City along the way. What was notable about their progression past those four clubs?

4. The team that beat them in that semi-final of 1972/73 also knocked Wolves out of the FA Cup in 1973/74 and 1976/77. Who were they?

5. Which club did Wolves meet in the FA Cup three seasons running in the 1970s? The seasons were 1974/75 when Wolves lost at home, 1975/76 when they drew away and won the replay, and 1976/77 when they again drew away and won the replay.

6. Which club knocked Wolves out of the FA Cup in 1977/78 and 1978/79, both times on their way to the final?

7. When Wolves won the League Cup in 1973/74, they beat just one club who finished above them in the league that year. Who were they?

8. Wolves' first-ever opponents in the League Cup back in 1966/67 got their revenge on them for that defeat by knocking Wolves out of the competition in 1975/76. Who were they?

9. Wolves won the League Cup again in 1979/80, but it proved something of a marathon. How many games did it take to win the trophy?

10. In winning that trophy, Wolves were taken to three games in the round before the semi-final, Wolves finally getting through on a neutral ground. Who put up a good fight before going down and on which ground did Wolves finally get through?

QUIZ No. 71

WOLVES IN CUP COMPETITIONS – THE 1980s

1. The decade began with a great FA Cup run to the semi-final where they forced a 2-2 draw with Spurs before losing the replay. Which two players scored their goals in the first tie?

2. Wolves got to that semi-final the hard way. Including that semi-final, they drew four times in the FA Cup that season, needing replays to get past Stoke City, Watford and Middlesbrough. The fifth round was the only time that they won through after one game, beating which Welsh club 3-1 at Molineux?

3. The rest of the decade told a terrible story in cup competitions. Counting both the FA Cup and League Cup produces 20 chances to progress past the first match each time. How many times did Wolves go out at the first attempt in either of these competitions?

4. Which club knocked Wolves out of the League Cup on two occasions in the 1980s, firstly in 1981/82 and then again in 1989/90?

5. It felt like a new low had been reached when a club not a million miles from Molineux dumped Wolves out of the League Cup and finished above them in the league in 1985/86. Which club must have enjoyed it no end?

6. Which club did Wolves knock out of the League Cup in 1989/90, having previously lost to them in the same competition on away goals in 1986/87?

7. In the FA Cup of 1983/84, Wolves were taken to a third match after two 1-1 draws. They lost the toss for staging the third match and the match itself by 3-0. Who knocked them out?

8. It was bad enough having to play in the first round of the FA Cup, but it was positively horrendous to go out to a non-league side, which Wolves did after three games in the 1986/87 season. Who knocked them out?

9. The answer to the previous question had given up their right to play on their own pitch in the first tie, which was drawn. There followed another Molineux draw before a return on the first ground again. Which league ground was therefore borrowed twice before this tie was concluded?

10. One man scored Wolves' last goal of the decade in both the FA Cup and the League Cup. Who was he?

QUIZ No. 72

WOLVES IN CUP COMPETITIONS – THE 1990s

1. In the first season of the decade, Wolves were disappointingly knocked out of both domestic Cup competitions at the first time of asking by two sides who share Wolves' colours. Who were they?

2. Wolves' biggest win in either competition also came early in the decade when they beat Shrewsbury Town in the first leg of a League Cup tie in 1991/92. What was the score?

3. On one occasion during the decade, in 1995/96, Wolves were knocked out of the League Cup by the eventual winners. Who were they?

4. Which three clubs with names beginning with the same letter as the Molineux club did they eliminate from the FA Cup during this decade?

5. In 1997/98, Wolves played 12 matches in cup competitions. Who, with four FA Cup goals and one League Cup goal, became their top scorer in both competitions for that season?

6. Who were the only club in this decade to knock Wolves out of the League Cup on two occasions, firstly in 1993/94, and again in 1996/97?

7. Which team, not currently in the league, that share Wolves' colours did they beat 5-0 in the second leg of a League Cup tie in the 1998/99 season?

8. Which club knocked Wolves out of the FA Cup in successive seasons in 1997/98 and 1998/99?

9. Which London club did Wolves knock out of both competitions in this decade, both times after a replay?

10. Who were the only club in this decade that lost and won an FA Cup tie against Wolves?

QUIZ No. 73

WOLVES IN THE LEAGUE - 1888-1915

1. When the Football League was formed in 1888, Wolves were one of the 12 founder members. In that first season of the 11 grounds they visited in the league, only two required a southerly journey. Which two clubs were involved?

2. What was the highest league position in top-flight football that Wolves attained in the period in question?

3. In 1895/96, the league expanded to 16 clubs. Wolves narrowly missed relegation by a single point due to winning their last two matches of the season, both at home against Lancashire clubs that start with the same letter. Who were they?

4. Two prolific goalscorers for Wolves, one in the late 19th century and the other in the early years of the 20th century, shared the first three letters of their names. They both ended up top Wolves scorer on four occasions, and shared it jointly as well. Who were they?

5. On 1 January 1900, Wolves travelled in a north-easterly direction and won 2-1 on a ground that had been opened the previous season. Which ground was it?

6. In which season did Wolves experience relegation for the first time?

7. In Division Two for the first time, Wolves started to meet teams with unfamiliar names. They played against two clubs with names beginning with 'G' who have not played league football for a long time, one failing to be re-elected in 1912 and the other resigning after World War One. Who were they?

8. Birmingham, before the 'City' was added, were the last visitors to Molineux before the war on 19 April 1915. The game was drawn 0-0, but why would Birmingham have been happier with their afternoon's work than Wolves?

9. In their final pre-war season, Wolves finished in their highest Division Two league position thus far. In what position did they finish?

10. Wolves drew 2-2 away to a Lancastrian club in their final match before war intervened. It was against a club George Best played for many years later. Who were they?

QUIZ No. 74

WOLVES IN THE LEAGUE - 1919-39

1. There was still a little aggression left over after World War One. On 18 October 1919, when Wolves lost 1-0 at home to Bury at Molineux, the crowd got somewhat irate over a refereeing decision and the official was knocked over in the melee. Wolves were ordered to play their ensuing home matches against Barnsley and Stockport County on 29 November and 5 December away from Molineux. On which ground did those games take place?

2. In season 1922/23, Wolves reached a low point in their history when they were relegated to Division Three North for the first time. A bad start did not help. What month were we in when Wolves won for the first time that season?

3. Wolves stayed just one season at that level before gaining promotion as champions in 1923/24. How many of their 21 home games did they lose?

4. Wolves finally returned to the top flight as champions in 1931/32. They lost just once at Molineux in the league that season. Who beat them?

5. They put numerous teams to the sword that season, scoring 115 times in 42 matches, with nearly two thirds of them coming at Molineux. How many did the home crowd see there that season from the home side?

6. In the last two completed seasons before war intervened again, Wolves finished runners-up in the top division. Which two teams denied them the title?

7. Since going up in 1931/32, Wolves never failed to reach double figures in league wins at Molineux in any completed season up to World War Two. True or false?

8. In 1937/38, they would have been champions for the first time in their history if they had won their final game. Instead, they lost 1-0 away to which club?

9. War caused the abandonment of the 1939/40 season after just three games. Wolves drew with both Arsenal and Grimsby Town before losing 2-1 away to the club that were top of the pile when the whole thing was brought to a shuddering halt. Who were they?

10. In the whole period, no Wolves player was a top scorer in any division. True or false?

WOLVES IN THE LEAGUE - 1946-60

1. Liverpool denying Wolves the league title on the last day of the 1946/47 season has been covered elsewhere. By what score had Wolves won at Anfield earlier that season?

2. Wolves came agonisingly close to that elusive first title once again in 1949/50. Going into the last game, three clubs could still win it. Wolves were one of them and did their bit by beating Birmingham City 6-1 at Molineux. Sunderland beat Chelsea 4-1 but the third club that were in with a chance won 5-1 at home to Aston Villa, a club unlikely to do Wolves any favours, and took the title on goal average. Who were they?

3. The day, for which the club had waited over 60 years, finally arrived in season 1953/54. It was particularly sweet because it stopped which club doing the first 'double' of the 20th century?

4. Wolves looked highly likely to retain their title in 1954/55, but lost a vital game 1-0 at Chelsea in front of a 75,000 crowd in April that effectively decided the destination of the title. Chelsea's goal came from the penalty spot after which Wolves player punched the ball from under his cross-bar to save a certain goal?

5. In 1957/58, Wolves struck gold again when they won the league by five points. They got off to a great start by winning how many games in a row at Molineux from the start of the season?

6. This time, Wolves did retain the title, winning it by six points. In a tremendous run-in they lost just once in their last 17 games. It was to the club that finished runners-up. Who were they?

7. Who was the only player to be sole top goalscorer for Wolves three seasons in a row in the period from 1946 to 1960?

8. Wolves' total of 64 points in 1957/58 had equalled Manchester United's total for the 1956/57 season, and had only been bettered once previously by which club in 1930/31?

9. Dennis Wilshaw made a dream debut for Wolves on 12 March 1949, scoring all three goals at Molineux in Wolves' 3-0 win over which club?

10. The first season back after the war was the only time a Wolves player was the league's top goalscorer. He scored 37 goals. Who was he?

QUIZ No. 76

WOLVES IN THE LEAGUE – 1960s

1. After the greatest decade in the club's history there appeared little concern at the start of the 1960s. 1960/61 saw them finish third, once again scoring more than 100 goals. Which London club did they beat 5-3 at home and 5-1 away?

2. In that 1960/61 season, Wolves won 17 of their 21 home games. Their only two defeats came at the hands of London clubs who each scored four times at Molineux in winning 4-0 and 4-2. Who were these two clubs?

3. Who was the only Wolves player in the 1960s to not miss a league game in two successive seasons? Those seasons were 1968/69 and 1969/70.

4. Who were the only two Wolves players to be the club's leading league goalscorers on more than one occasion in the decade?

5. 1964/65 was a disastrous season for the Wolves and culminated in relegation from the top flight, something that had last happened in 1905/06. The only speck of light in a very dark tunnel was the identity of the club which fell through the trap door with them. Who were they?

6. In their first season in Division Two, Wolves finished sixth, the highlight of the season being an 8-2 home win on 27 November 1965 against a club they often chalked up a lot of goals against. Who were they?

7. Wolves returned to the top table on gaining promotion at the end of 1966/67 and would have gone up as champions if they had drawn their last game of the season in London on 13 May 1967. Which club beat them 4-1 to put an end to that possibility?

8. In their first season back in the First Division, Wolves failed to score more than three goals in any league game except one. It came on 6 April 1968 when they beat which Midlands club 6-1 at Molineux?

9. The closing two seasons of the decade saw Wolves managing to keep their heads above the water line, although 1969/70 witnessed an alarming slide from a promising position going into the new year. Wolves had opened the season with four straight wins but went into a tail-spin, their last win of the season coming on 24 January. How many games did they go without a win from that day to the season's end?

10. Which Wolves player scored more league goals in the decade than anyone else despite never scoring the most in any individual season?

WOLVES IN THE LEAGUE - 1970s

1. The two league seasons that Wolves would have enjoyed the most in the 1970s were 1970/71, when they finished fourth in Division One, and 1976/77, when they were promoted back in to that division after relegation in 1975/76. Each of those seasons comprised 42 matches and Wolves won the same number of matches both times. How many was that?

2. In May 1972, Leeds United came to Molineux hoping to get the win that would clinch the league and cup double. They had won the FA Cup on the previous Saturday, just two days earlier. 53,379 fans saw Molineux prove a bridge too far as Wolves ran out 2-1 winners. With Liverpool dropping a point at Highbury, Derby became champions. Which two men scored for Wolves?

3. Over the decade, John Richards was top league scorer five times, while Derek Dougan and Kenny Hibbitt shared four equally between them. Who, in 1970/71, was top scorer in that first season of the decade?

4. On 27 January 1973, Molineux witnessed a 2-1 Wolves win over the eventual champions Liverpool. Which Liverpool player who later joined Wolves scored one of their goals that day by putting the ball in his own net?

5. Liverpool came to Molineux for their last match of the 1975/76 season needing to at least draw to land the title. Wolves led between the 13th and the 76th minutes but eventually went down 3-1. Which club which has never won the league was denied it that season by Liverpool's comeback?

6. Wolves went straight back up as champions in 1976/77, winning away by 6-1 and 5-1 during the season. Which two clubs from the west of the country were beaten on their own grounds in those matches?

7. Who, as far as can be known, on 15 November 1975 scored the fastest-ever goal by a Wolves player when his '12th second' strike set up a 5-1 win over Burnley at Turf Moor?

8. Wolves, in 1976/77, had four players who appeared in every league game. Three of them have names beginning with a 'P' while the fourth left Wolves for a record fee three years down the line. Who were the four players?

9. Which Wolves player scored five of their eight goals when they beat West Brom and Nottingham Forest by 4-2 and 4-0 in successive games in the 1970/71 season?

10. Which two clubs, one from Yorkshire and the other from Lancashire, went down with Wolves when they were relegated from the top flight in 1975/76?

QUIZ No. 78

WOLVES IN THE LEAGUE - 1980s

1. Which Wolves defender was the only man in this decade to twice have an ever-present league season? He achieved this feat in 1982/83 and 1984/85?

2. In successive seasons, 1981/82 and 1982/83, one Wolves goalkeeper followed another in playing in every league game. The two men's names began with the same letter. Who were they?

3. He played just nine times for Wolves and scored just one goal. But what a goal it was! In a season so miserable that Wolves won just six of their 42 matches and were relegated from the top flight, they actually beat the eventual champions 1-0 at Anfield on 14 January 1984. Who scored that goal?

4. Wolves fans must have thought that 1983/84 was about as bad as it could get, but they soon had to think again after finding that playing in the Second Division in 1984/85 was not much easier and at the end of it they had fallen to an even lower level. The nightmare could be summed up not by the fact that their top league scorer award was shared by Alan Ainscow, Tony Evans and Mark Buckland, but by the number of goals each of them managed. How many was it?

5. Earlier, in 1981/82, Wolves had experienced relegation from the top flight, but bounced back the following season, going up with runaway champions Queens Park Rangers. Who topped the scoring list for the club in both the relegation and promotion season?

6. 1985/86 was probably the worst season in the club's history and, at the end of it, they were relegated to the fourth tier of English football for the first time. If you know the price of Lester Piggott's first Derby winner, Never Say Die, in 1954, then you will know how many players Wolves threw at their problems without success in 1985/86. How many was it?

7. Fortunately, a saviour was on hand in the shape of Steve Bull. His goals steadied the ship in 1986/87 and helped Wolves to promotion the following season. In fact, in 1987/88 he was top scorer over all four divisions, his 44 outings yielding how many goals?

8. Which Wolves player occupied second place behind Steve Bull in four successive seasons in the late 1980s?

9. What was the link between Wolves' opponents Preston North End, Mansfield Town, Fulham and Bury in the promotion out of Division Three in 1988/89?

10. Which team from the west of the country were the only one to come away from Molineux with all of the points in 1988/89?

QUIZ No. 79

WOLVES IN THE LEAGUE – 1990s

1. In the first season of the new decade, Wolves broke their club record for the number of draws in a season. How many of the 46 games did they draw?

2. One Watford player was particularly kind to Wolves at the start of the decade. He put through his own net at Molineux on 18 January 1992 when Wolves won 3-0, and then in the following season repeated the trick when Wolves won 4-1 at Watford in the FA Cup third round. Who was he?

3. Which player scored the first and last league goals of the season for Wolves in 1991/92, the first coming at Watford and the last at home to Middlesbrough?

4. 20 February 1999 saw the only occasion during the 1990s when a crowd in excess of 40,000 watched Wolves in a league game. The figure was 41,268 and Wolves lost the match 2-1. On which ground did it occur?

5. Steve Bull monopolised the leading scorer category, winning it six times. Who was the only other Wolves player to win it more than once over the decade?

6. It is hard to believe, but it appears that Wolves scored from the penalty spot just once in the decade. This came in a 2-2 draw with Port Vale at Molineux on 23 October 1999. Who took it?

7. Which player helped to sink Wolves' hopes in the 1996/97 play-offs by scoring against them, before joining the club the following season?

8. In the first two years of the decade, five players with surnames starting with a 'B' scored for Wolves in the league. Obviously, one of them is Steve Bull. Who are the other four?

9. If you put together the surnames of two Wolves players who scored for them in the league in 1995/96 then you produce a decathlete with two Olympic gold medals to his name. Who was he?

10. One team met Wolves twice on the opening day of the season over the decade. Wolves drew 2-2 away to them in August 1995, before beating them 2-0 at Molineux in August 1998. Who were they?

QUIZ No. 80

WOLVES VERSUS
WEST BROMWICH ALBION

1. Sadly, Wolves have won only one FA Cup tie against West Bromwich Albion. It happened in the sixth round of the 1948/49 season on the road to Wembley when they beat them 1-0 at Molineux with whose goal?

2. 1937/38 was a crazy season where the champions and the bottom club were separated by just 16 points. Why might Wolves have been more than usually pleased with their 2-1 win over Albion on 2 May?

3. 2006/07 was a painful season for Wolves fans because West Brom knocked them out of the FA Cup, beat them in the play-offs and won the league fixture at the Hawthorns. The only piece of a silver lining in a very large dark cloud came when Wolves won the league match at Molineux 1-0. Who got the vital goal?

4. As you may know, Wolves and West Brom were two of the 12 clubs that formed the Football League in the 1888/89 season. Obviously, they met six times in the league over the first three seasons. How many of these six did Wolves win?

5. What links the following players: Teddy Pheasant, Cecil Shaw, Don Goodman and Ally Robertson?

6. Wolves' biggest hammering of West Brom came at Molineux in the old First Division on 16 March 1963. Terry Wharton got a hat-trick in the game. By what score did Wolves prevail?

7. In the first game between the clubs for three years in the second match of the 1967/68 season, a crowd of 52,438 turned up at Molineux and witnessed an exciting game that ended in the same score as the Molineux match two years earlier. What was the score?

8. Who scored home and away for Wolves when he played against Albion for the first time in 1989/90, Wolves winning both encounters 2-1?

9. In the win at the Hawthorns, two ex-Albion men got the Wolves goals. I expect that you have already worked out who was responsible for the answer to the previous question but who was the other ex-West Brom man to score in that game?

10. What was unique about the two league matches between the clubs in season 1979/80 in the old First Division?

QUIZ No. 81

WOLVES - SEASON 2000/01

1. The new millennium began with a season of mid-table mediocrity. On 13 August Wolves started with a 1-1 draw with Sheffield Wednesday at Molineux. Who scored their goal?

2. Before August was out, someone had scored a hat-trick against Wolves. It came in the first half at Fratton Park on the 28th of the month in a 3-1 defeat to Portsmouth. Who scored it?

3. Perhaps the best moments of the season came close together on 18 March and 1 April. Firstly, West Brom were beaten 3-1 at Molineux, while the 'April fools' turned out to be Birmingham City, who lost 1-0 on their own turf. The same man grabbed two against Albion and the winner in the very first minute at St Andrew's. Who was he?

4. The FA Cup started promisingly enough when which Midlands club were dumped out on their own pitch 1-0 with Adam Proudlock netting an 87th-minute winner?

5. Wolves made a spirited comeback at the first hurdle in the League Cup when, trailing 2-0 on aggregate away from home at half time in the second leg, they scored three times to turn the tie on its head. Wolves had beaten a team playing in their colours. Who were they?

6. One player appeared from the start in all 46 league games, while another started 44 and came off the bench in the other two. Who were they?

7. Eventually, Wolves were knocked out of the League Cup by Grimsby Town, while the team that put paid to their FA Cup hopes were one of the few clubs to follow them in the alphabet. Who were they?

8. Who were the only two players to score for Wolves in the league, the FA Cup and the League Cup?

9. During the course of the season, two ex-Spurs players whose names begin with the same letter turned out for the Wanderers. Who were they?

10. A 1-1 draw at Molineux started the season and it was brought to a close at the same venue on 6 May with another 1-1 draw, this time against Queens Park Rangers. Which defender scored Wolves' final goal of the season?

WOLVES - SEASON 2001/02

1. Despite a ten-point lead over the third-placed club at one stage of the season, Wolves blew it and their failure was rendered ten times worse by the identities of the two clubs that managed to get above them and in the process reach the Premier League, one by finishing second to the champions and the other through the play-offs. Sorry, but who were they?

2. On the opening day, 11 August at Molineux, Wolves found themselves 2-0 down before an encouraging fight-back, with goals from Shaun Newton and Cedric Roussel got them a point from a 2-2 draw. Which southern club went home with one point instead of three?

3. On 18 September, Wolves won 3-2 away in a match where both teams scored in the last minute. The same opponents went on to turn the tables on Wolves by knocking them out of the FA Cup 1-0 at Molineux in the third round. Who were they?

4. Whose hat-trick on 27 November secured a 4-1 home win for Wolves against Barnsley?

5. In the League Cup, Wolves lost 2-1 at home to Swindon Town on 22 August. Which defender therefore became their only goalscorer in that season's competition?

6. On 13 October, an Adam Proudlock hat-trick helped Wolves to a 3-0 win in Yorkshire. Who did they beat?

7. During the season, Wolves were prolific scorers away from home, finding the net 43 times on their travels. This total was ten more than they achieved at Molineux and was surpassed by just one club, the eventual runaway champions. Who were they?

8. Wolves had the better of their encounters with local rivals Walsall, winning home and away by the same score. What was it?

9. Which Scot who became Wolves' 'Player of the Year' at the season's end got the winner against Millwall, one of his former clubs, at Molineux in that season?

10. Wolves went out at the semi-final stage in the play-offs, and their conquerors have been covered elsewhere. Dean Sturridge scored in the away leg, but who scored the only goal of the game in the second leg at Molineux?

QUIZ No. 83

WOLVES - SEASON 2002/03

1. Wolves reached the promised land at last, despite falling from third place to fifth, gaining the same number of points as in the previous season when they failed to get promotion. How many points?

2. An ex-Wanderer came back to bite Wolves on 19 September by scoring twice for Crystal Palace when they won 4-2 at Selhurst Park. Who was he?

3. In February, Wolves won two away games, scoring four goals on each occasion. Which clubs were beaten 4-0 and 4-2?

4. Wolves exacted revenge on Crystal Palace for that earlier 4-2 defeat by winning 4-0 on 1 March at Molineux. Who was their hat-trick hero on that day?

5. Which club did Wolves hammer mercilessly in their two league encounters, winning 6-0 at home and 4-0 away, assisted on the latter occasion by a treble from Nathan Blake?

6. Wolves reached the play-offs with a great run. How many of their last 16 league games did they lose?

7. Which club did Wolves beat 3-1 over two legs in the play-off semi-final?

8. A promising FA Cup run was ended in quarter-final defeat at Southampton. Wolves had previously knocked out Newcastle United, Leicester City and Rochdale. Who scored in all three of those wins?

9. Which two Wolves defenders missed just five league games between them and were both included in the PFA Divisional Team of the Year?

10. Molineux also saw an award for Jonathan Calderwood at the season's end. What was it for?

WOLVES - SEASON 2003/04

1. Losing a pre-season friendly 6-1 to a side in the fourth tier of English football was an ominous precursor to a season that brought relegation from the top flight. Which seaside town club beat them?

2. Which two clubs beginning with the same letter were relegated along with Wolves, all three managing 33 points?

3. A dose of reality was not long in coming, Blackburn Rovers inflicting a 5-1 defeat on Wolves on the opening day at Ewood Park. Which ex-Spurs player got their consolation goal?

4. It was October before Wolves won a league game, 1-0 at home to Manchester City. Who scored that much-needed goal?

5. The season's most exciting and rewarding moment came in a game that looked pretty bleak at half time. It was at Molineux on 25 October and Leicester City led 3-0 at the break. A great second-half fightback by the home side turned this around, however, and they won the game 4-3 with an 86th-minute winner by their eventual 'Player of the Year'. Who was he?

6. Wolves had a big scare in the FA Cup third round when an 89th-minute Alex Rae goal saved their bacon at which non-league club?

7. Which outfield player was on the pitch in all 38 league games?

8. In both the FA Cup and the League Cup, Wolves eventually went out to London clubs. Which two clubs were involved?

9. A Wolves defender experienced contrasting situations on two visits to the capital during the league season. Against Arsenal at Highbury he scored an own goal but later versus Chelsea at Stamford Bridge he scored in the right end. Who was he?

10. On 6 December, which ex-Wolves player scored a hat-trick against them when Spurs beat Wolves 5-2 at White Hart Lane?

QUIZ No. 85

WOLVES - SEASON 2004/05

1. Which Wolves manager lost his job after defeat by Gillingham on 30 October, and who eventually replaced him?

2. Which Wolves player grabbed a 90th-minute leveller for them in a 3-3 draw at Wigan on 11 September?

3. Which Wolves defender who appeared in 11 league games was the only squad member to be born in Wolverhampton?

4. On 27 November, Wolves drew 3-3 away to a Yorkshire club with whom they had also drawn 3-3 on the same ground two seasons earlier. Who were their opponents?

5. Between 11 December and 1 January, Wolves had five league fixtures. They were against Watford, Crewe Alexandra, Cardiff City, Brighton & Hove Albion and Plymouth Argyle. What was odd about these five matches?

6. In the FA Cup, Wolves beat a London team from their own division in the third round before going out in round four to another London club, this time from the Premiership. Who were their two opponents?

7. In the League Cup they won 4-2 in Lancashire against a team from the fourth tier of English football, before going out in the next round to another club from that county, this time from their own division. Who were the two teams they played against?

8. Who was the only man to score for Wolves in both the FA Cup and the League Cup in 2004/05?

9. In this season, Wolves created a new club record for the number of draws they were involved in. Of their 46 league games, how many finished level?

10. A tough one to finish with! Two players scored winning goals for Wolves during the season, but these proved to be the only ones either of them scored for the club. The first man got the winner against Nottingham Forest on 6 November at Molineux and then, later in the season on 30 April, the other got a late winner at Reading. Who were the two players?

QUIZ No. 86

WOLVES - SEASON 2005/06

1. After Wolves finished the season one place off the play-offs, which manager of theirs resigned at the season's end?

2. Which Wolves player scored a hat-trick in a 3-1 home win over Queens Park Rangers on 30 August?

3. Which on-loan Spurs player was among the scorers in a 3-0 win at Derby County on 18 November?

4. In the domestic cup competitions, Wolves went out to Manchester United and Watford. Their only FA Cup goal came in the third round when Leon Clarke's strike beat which club from the South West?

5. Which midfielder got a late winner for Wolves at Molineux against Luton Town in January and then, on Valentine's Day, got another winner, this time at Burnley?

6. Who was the only Wolves player to make the PFA 'Divisional Team of the Year'?

7. Which Wolves player who was the club's 'Player of the Year' scored from the penalty spot against Brighton, Cardiff and Ipswich during the season?

8. Which on-loan Arsenal player scored in Wolves' 3-2 win at Hull City on 25 February?

9. Whose goal at Molineux against Leeds United on 17 December proved to be the only one of the game?

10. Which veteran with 30 England caps to his name played 24 times for Wolves in the league during the season, scoring in the 5-1 win over Chester City in the first round of the League Cup?

WOLVES - SEASON 2006/07

1. Mick McCarthy became Wolves manager at the start of the season and they reached the play-offs under him. Where had his previous term of management been?

2. During the season, Wolves beat Ipswich Town, Colchester and West Brom at home and Leeds United away, all by 1-0. One man scored all four of those winning goals. Who was he?

3. Which Wolves player scored twice at Molineux on 28 October against Sheffield Wednesday, and then bagged another brace when Southend United were the visitors for the next home fixture?

4. Which Wolves defender proved his attacking credentials in no uncertain terms when he got a very welcome late leveller at Birmingham City, followed it up with a winner at Southend, and then, in the new year, got a last-minute equaliser in a 2-2 draw with Norwich City at Molineux?

5. Which player, who later signed for Wolves, scored against them when they went down 2-1 at Colchester on 30 December?

6. Wolves' problems with West Brom in the 2006/07 season have been covered elsewhere, but which player proved to be a particular thorn in Wolves' side by scoring against them in both legs of the play-offs as well as in the FA Cup tie that Albion won 3-0 at Molineux?

7. Which newcomer advertised his presence by scoring the three winning goals in victories over QPR at Loftus Road, Leeds United at Molineux and Norwich City at Carrow Road, all by 1-0?

8. Who was the only player to score for Wolves in both the FA Cup and the play-offs?

9. Who, having started all 46 league games, was voted Wolves' 'Player of the Year'?

10. Prior to the eventual play-off disappointment, Wolves finished the league season on a high note. Going behind in the third minute away from home, they ran out 4-1 winners. Which Midlands club did they beat in that final game?

WOLVES - SEASON 2007/08

1. A frustrating end to the season saw Wolves miss out on the play-offs on goal difference. They shared their 70 points total with another club, but ended up a goal light. Which club denied Wolves a shout in the play-offs?

2. Which Wolves defender who had joined the club from Sunderland scored winning goals against Coventry City, Barnsley and Scunthorpe United in the league and against Cambridge United in the FA Cup?

3. Wolves' biggest Molineux league win was by 3-0 and their biggest Molineux defeat was also by that score. Two clubs with names beginning with the same letter, one from London and the other from Wales, were involved. Who were they?

4. A key point in the season proved to be the signing in January of Sylvan Ebanks-Blake, who eventually topped the league goalscorers chart for the whole division with 23; 12 of those were for Wolves. For whom had he scored the other 11?

5. Who saved a point for Wolves with a goal in the 96th minute of the home game with Queens Park Rangers on 22 March, making the final outcome a 3-3 draw?

6. The following week, on 29 March, the finish of the game between Charlton Athletic and Wolves provided a few thrills. Charlton made it 2-2 in the 92nd minute before which midfielder won it for Wolves in the 94th minute?

7. Whose 87th-minute winner for Wolves in the season's final game against Plymouth Argyle at Molineux on 4 May proved to be his last goal for the club?

8. Ebanks-Blake scored his first Wolves goal in a 2-0 away win on 19 January. Who did they beat?

9. Wolves went out of the League Cup after extra time to Morecambe of League Two. Which Yorkshire club had they defeated 2-1 at Molineux to reach that stage?

10. For the second season running, the Wolves 'Player of the Year' occupied the same position on the field, the new recipient of the award getting his chance to play in all 46 league games because a serious injury to the previous winner had put him out for the season. Who won the 'Player of the Year' accolade?

WOLVES - SEASON 2008/09

1. Wolves went up as champions despite having a sticky patch in the middle of the season. Before the dodgy spell, they had a run of winning games which they repeated later in the season. How many successive times did they win each time?

2. Promotion was clinched on 18 April when an Ebanks-Blake goal was enough to beat which London club at Molineux?

3. The title itself came with a 1-1 draw at Oakwell versus Barnsley when someone who played only a handful of games for Wolves equalised in the 84th minute. It was his only goal for the club, but a memorable one! Who was he?

4. One of the season's strangest events saw two Wolves goalkeepers concede own goals within three weeks of each other. The first one came on 30 September at home to Reading, and the second at Norwich on 21 October. Who were the two goalkeepers?

5. Sylvan Ebanks-Blake's 25 league goals brought him the 'Divisional Player of the Year' award, but the Wolves 'Player of the Year' went to a defender who missed just one of the 46 league games. Who was he?

6. Ebanks-Blake and Iwelumo both scored hat-tricks in the league campaign, the former's coming in a 3-3 draw at Molineux, and the latter's in a 3-1 win in Lancashire. Who were their two opponents?

7. In the FA Cup, Wolves started out with a very satisfying 2-0 win at Birmingham before going out to Middlesbrough in the fourth round. Which Wolves player scored in both matches?

8. Before being knocked out of the League Cup in the next round on penalties by Rotherham, Wolves were taken tò extra time at Molineux before they saw off their fourth-tier opponents from Lancashire by 3-2. Which club put up a good fight before their exit from the competition?

9. Two clubs whose names begin with the same letter were promoted alongside Wolves. Who were they?

10. On 3 May, Molineux was in a celebratory mood for the final game against Doncaster Rovers. Whose last-minute winner made the presentation of the trophy moments later feel even better?

QUIZ No. 90

WOLVES - SEASON 2009/10

1. Kevin Doyle became Wolves' most expensive purchase when they paid which club £6.5 million for his services?

2. On 19 August, Wolves won their first away match in the Premier League when an Andy Keogh goal gave them three points on whose ground?

3. Wolves did the league 'double' over two clubs during the season. It may help to say that they met each other in the 1962 FA Cup Final. Who were the two clubs?

4. Arsenal are always a tough team to beat without giving them a two-goal start, which was exactly what Wolves did on 7 December at Molineux, eventually going down 4-1. Which two players scored own goals, one of them redeeming himself by scoring at the right end in the last minute?

5. Why did Wolves manager Mick McCarthy get into hot water with the authorities after Wolves lost 3-0 to Manchester United at Old Trafford on 15 December?

6. Which goalkeeper played the most times in the league for Wolves in 2009/10?

7. In the FA Cup, Wolves went out in the fourth round after a replay against Crystal Palace. In the previous round, they had beaten Tranmere Rovers 1-0 at Prenton Park. Which player who joined Wolves from Gillingham came up with the winner?

8. On 13 March, when Wolves won 2-1 at Burnley, they were the beneficiaries of an own goal by a Burnley player who shares his name with a northern football club. Who was he?

9. Which midfielder, with a total of 34, made the most starts for
    Wolves in the league?

10. Wolves celebrated their first survival of a season in the top flight for
    29 years with a final-day 2-1 win over Sunderland at Molineux on
    9 May. Which Frenchman got the final goal of the season that won
    the game with 12 minutes remaining?

QUIZ No. 91

WOLVES - SEASON 2010/11

1. It was a tough old time in 2010/11 and Wolves were grateful to still be in the division by the end of it, finishing one place out of the bottom three. How many points did they have in hand of the relegated club in 18th place?

2. A high point of the league season was a 1-0 win over Liverpool at Anfield on 29 December. Who got their winner in the 56th minute?

3. In early January, Chelsea were beaten at Molineux by the same score of 1-0. Which Chelsea defender gave Wolves the perfect start with an own goal in the fifth minute?

4. Wolves' biggest win of the season came in an FA Cup third-round replay when they won 5-0 after a 2-2 away draw. Which Yorkshire club left Molineux knocked out of the competition?

5. Wolves were brought down to earth in the next round when which club came to Molineux and knocked them out 1-0?

6. Wolves shared seven goals in a game just once that season, on 15 January, when they were beaten 4-3 away from home. Who narrowly beat them and which pair of brothers scored against them in the game?

7. The season's biggest league win was a 4-0 victory at Molineux against one of the relegated clubs. Which one?

8. Wolves were unfortunately involved in the lowest Premier League attendance of the season of 14,042. On whose ground?

9. The latest winning goal which Wolves scored came in the 123rd minute of their League Cup tie against Southend United at Molineux. Whose late strike enabled them to win 2-1?

10. They went out of the League Cup to Manchester United but, in the previous round, they were taken to extra time by Notts County at Molineux before prevailing 4-2. Which man scored the two vital goals in extra time that decided the tie?

QUIZ No. 92

WOLVES - SEASON 2011/12

1. This season proved to be even tougher than the last, Wolves ending it at the bottom of the table. What was the highest position they attained during the season?

2. Which two Lancashire clubs whose names begin with the same letter were relegated with Wolves?

3. Before going out of the League Cup 5-2 at home to Manchester City, Wolves had beaten which London club 5-0 in that competition?

4. 50,000-plus crowds watched Wolves on three away grounds during the season. What were these three venues?

5. In the FA Cup, Wolves went out at the first obstacle after a replay against which local rivals?

6. The highest scoring game Wolves were involved in came when they recovered from two goals down to force a 4-4 draw away to which club?

7. Scoring goals was a major problem. In their league campaign, only one man got into double figures. Who was he?

8. Somewhat overworked, it was hardly surprising who won Wolves 'Player of the Year' award. Who was he?

9. Wolves conceded five goals on three occasions in the league. One was a 5-0 defeat at Fulham, while the other two came at Molineux when they lost 5-1 and 5-0 to which clubs?

10. Which Wolves manager was sacked after the 5-1 home defeat with 13 games of the season remaining?

QUIZ No. 93

WOLVES - SEASON 2012/13

1. A terrible season produced a second successive relegation. Who were the only club to finish below Wolves in the Championship table?

2. A small consolation could be had by their league double over which local rival?

3. Things were no better where the FA Cup was concerned. Wolves were eliminated in the third round by a non-league side. Who were they?

4. In the League Cup, Wolves progressed with some difficulty past Aldershot, then won at Northampton before finally succumbing heavily to Chelsea. Which one of those three clubs had they met in the same competition the previous year?

5. Who scored twice for Wolves in a 2-1 win at Blackpool before repeating the feat in the new year when they won 3-2 at Birmingham?

6. Two managers paid the price and were sacked. The first after the FA Cup defeat, while the second departed three days after relegation was confirmed. Who were the two managers?

7. On 26 January, Wolves were beaten 2-1 at home by Blackpool. Both goals for the visitors were scored by the son of a former Wolves player. Who got the Blackpool goals?

8. Which defender rescued a point for Wolves in the 92nd minute in a 3-3 draw at Molineux against Brighton on 10 November?

9. On 23 October, Wolves drew 2-2 at home to Bolton. One of the scorers for their opponents that day later joined Wolves. Who was he?

10. The Wolves player who got an added time leveller for them at home to Watford on 1 March went on to become their 'Player of the Year'. Who was he?

QUIZ No. 94

WOLVES - SEASON 2013/14

1. At last! A great year was crowned with the League One title and a new third-tier points record. How many?

2. Which manager guided them to their title?

3. On which London club's ground did Wolves clinch the title by winning 3-1?

4. During the season, Wolves broke the club's record by winning how many games in a row?

5. Which Wolves defender was on the field for 44 of their 46 matches that season?

6. There were quite a few to choose from when it came to announcing the 'Player of the Year' and the verdict went to Kevin McDonald. He was born in a town with a famous golf course. Which town was it?

7. Wolves went out at the first hurdle in both domestic cup competitions. In the FA Cup, they were beaten, after a replay, by a team in their division and in the League Cup by a team from the division below them. Which two teams were involved?

8. Molineux experienced the highest League One attendance of 30,110, which fortunately coincided with the highest aggregate score of the season when Wolves and Rotherham United shared ten goals on 18 April. What was the score?

9. On 23 August, Crawley Town were feeling good about their added-time equaliser at Molineux when whose penalty won it for Wolves even later into added time?

10. Wolves lost just two league games all season at Molineux. One of them came against MK Dons, but the other one would have hurt more because it came against close neighbours to the east. Who were they?

QUIZ No. 95

WOLVES - SEASON 2014/15

1. An excellent season saw newly promoted Wolves miss out on a play-off place on goal difference to two clubs. Who were they?

2. Wolves' top league goalscorer that season with 15 was also the only Wolves player to be chosen as part of the 'Championship team of the Season'. Who was he?

3. Wolves had an unfortunate run in the middle of the season that proved costly at the end of it. How many games in a row did they lose?

4. Kevin McDonald appeared in all 46 league matches for Wolves. True or false?

5. Who scored the winner for Wolves at Watford on Boxing Day?

6. Benik Afobe's goals in the second half of the season were a real tonic for Wolves. He came to the club in the January transfer window from which club?

7. On 6 April, perhaps the season's most exciting game took place at Molineux. Wolves won it 4-3 with a headed goal two minutes from the end. Who did they beat and who scored the goal?

8. On 10 February, one of Wolves goals in a 4-1 win at Huddersfield Town was an own goal. The player that scored it ended up at Molineux the following season and his career has gone from strength to strength since then. Who was he?

9. In the early stages of the season, Wolves experienced two 3-3 draws away to southern clubs, one from the capital and the other a few miles west of it. Which two clubs were they?

10. The previous season had seen Wolves chalk up nine goals over the two games played against this club. That clearly didn't dull their appetite and the season's biggest win, 5-0 at Molineux on 21 February, came against that same club. Who were they?

QUIZ No. 96

WOLVES - SEASON 2015/16

1. After going so close to the play-offs the previous season, this one was something of a let-down, perhaps personified best by the number of 0-0 Molineux draws. How many were there?

2. Things started well enough when an Afobe goal in the 29th minute was the prelude to a 2-1 win in Lancashire on the season's opening day. Who did they beat?

3. There was eventual League Cup disappointment with a 3-0 defeat at Middlesbrough. Before that though, Wolves had knocked out two teams that share their colours. Who were they?

4. One Wolves player came off the bench 16 times for them during the season as well as making ten starts. He is perhaps best remembered for an 85th-minute winner against Charlton Athletic on 29 August. Who was he?

5. Having already won at Craven Cottage in September, Wolves completed the double over Fulham with a 3-2 Molineux win on 12 January. Which new recruit from Legia Warsaw scored twice in the game?

6. As well as landing the Wolves 'Player of the Year' award, he also secured three points for the Wanderers with a 94th-minute winner against Bristol City on 8 March, at Molineux. Who was he?

7. In a disappointing season, at least one player got into double figures on the goals front in the league. True or false?

8. Which Wolves defender missed just four league games all season, the best record of any Wolves player?

9. The next most consistent player, with 38 league games to his credit, was also a defender who, on 19 March at Turf Moor, stunned the Burnley crowd with an equaliser for Wolves in the 92nd minute. Who was he?

10. Wolves lost 1-0 away to a London club in the FA Cup third round. The club that beat them then accounted for Liverpool and Blackburn Rovers before going out in the quarter-final after a replay against the eventual winners Manchester United. Who knocked Wolves out?

QUIZ No. 97

WOLVES - SEASON 2016/17

1. Wolves were hugely disappointing at Molineux where their league losses reached double figures. They moved away from any real threat of relegation but nevertheless there were three managerial casualties by the season's end. Who were they?

2. During the season, Wolves endured a bad run of successive defeats, but put it right with an equal number of successive wins later in the season. What was that number?

3. On 24 September, Wolves beat Brentford 3-1 at Molineux, two of the goals coming from someone who did not score again. Who was he?

4. Two penalties that were both converted helped Wolves to avoid defeat in one game and win another. The first got Wolves a 1-1 draw at Villa Park on 15 October, Villa's goal also coming from the spot. The second came in a 3-2 Boxing Day win over Bristol City at Molineux. Which two players took the penalties?

5. Which Yorkshire club did Wolves beat 3-1 away yet lose to 4-0 at home?

6. On 14 January, Wolves beat Aston Villa 1-0 at Molineux. Who endeared himself to the Wolves fans with the winning goal?

7. In the League Cup, before finally bowing out at Newcastle, Wolves beat two clubs from the fourth tier of English football 2-1 at Molineux. The clubs' names start with the same letter. Who were they?

8. Within five days in March the Wolves away support was treated to two wins in a row in West London. They came on the 14th and the 18th of the month, the first by 2-1 and the second by 3-1. Which two sides were beaten?

9. The highlight of the season was a 2-1 win over Liverpool at Anfield in the FA Cup fourth round. Richard Stearman's goal in the first minute provided the platform, but who scored the other goal?

10. Which London club brought them down to earth by beating them 2-0 in the fifth round of the FA Cup?

WOLVES – SEASON 2017/18

1. This was a great season, culminating in the Championship title, with 99 points. It was welcome particularly at Molineux, where Wolves had lost 11 times in the previous campaign, but had now reduced that number to just two. Fellow promotion winners Cardiff City were one of the sides to win there. Which other Midlands club also managed the feat?

2. Who scored the winner in a 1-0 win over Middlesbrough on the first day of the season at Molineux and went on to score three of the first four Wolves goals on home soil in that season?

3. Wolves went out of the FA Cup in the third round, losing 2-1 at Swansea. Who, therefore, became their only goalscorer in the competition in that season?

4. Which club from Lancashire did Wolves hammer 5-1 at home and 4-0 away?

5. Yorkshire didn't escape either. Which club with the same coloured shirts as the answer to the last question lost 4-1 and 3-0 to Wolves during the league season?

6. In the League Cup, Wolves played in four games without conceding a goal, before going out unluckily on penalties at Manchester City after giving a great account of themselves on the night. Which three clubs, two from the West Country and one from the south coast, did they beat to reach that stage?

7. In an exciting finale to the home league fixture with Barnsley, the visitors equalised in the 91st minute. Who netted the decider for Wolves two minutes later?

8. Towards the end of the season, Wolves travelled to Cardiff, who were the only team who stood between them and the title. A 1-0 win saw wild jubilation from the Wolves camp and some anger from the home side. What events transpired in the last few minutes to cause the Cardiff bench and players to lose their heads?

9. John Ruddy missed just one of the 46 games that Wolves played in the league season. Who stood in for him on that one occasion?

10. Ruddy was one of the Wolves men that made the PFA 'Team of the Year' for the Championship. Which two other players were selected?

QUIZ No. 99

WOLVES - SEASON 2018/19

1. In Wolves' first away game back in the Premier League, on 18 August against Leicester City at the King Power Stadium, which member of the home side was sent off?

2. On 1 September, Wolves recorded their first away win of the season against West Ham United at a ground which should have been called 'The Bobby Moore Stadium'. Who got the only goal of the game?

3. Which Wolves player was unfortunate to put through his own net in successive games against Manchester City and Leicester City, and then do it a third time in March against Burnley?

4. Wolves eventually went out of the League Cup on penalties to Leicester City, but who did they beat 2-0 away from home in the previous round?

5. Which club did Wolves beat 2-1 at Molineux in both the Premier League and the FA Cup?

6. Wolves met Leicester City three times over the course of the season, the most exciting contest being the one at Molineux on 19 January. The score had happened between them on the same ground a few years before. What was it?

7. After eliminating Liverpool from the FA Cup in the third round, Wolves made the short journey to Shrewsbury and a potential banana skin in the fourth round. Sure enough, they found themselves 2-0 down before Jimenez got one back in the 75th minute. Whose 93rd minute leveller saved their blushes and brought Shrewsbury back to Molineux?

8. Who scored Wolves' last home goal of the season at Molineux on 4 May when Fulham were beaten 1-0?

9. Which Newcastle United defender was sent off when Wolves won 2-1 at St James' Park on 9 December?

10. Wolves made a spirited run to the semi-final stage of the FA Cup, but their progress was surprisingly ended when they surrendered a two-goal lead to Watford. Which club did they knock out in the quarter-final to reach that stage?

QUIZ No. 100

WOLVES - SEASON 2019/20

1. For the second season running, Wolves finished a very respectable seventh in the Premier League despite playing enough matches to bring anyone to their knees. Their expansive, attacking football was widely admired, but nevertheless they didn't manage to score more than three times in any of their 38 league games. True or false?

2. Dendoncker, Moutinho, Jimenez and Neves were all on the pitch at some point in all 38 league games, but only two players started every league game. Who were they?

3. Wolves did the league 'double' over five clubs. One came from the Midlands, one from the south coast, one from London, one from the east of the country and one from Lancashire. Who were the five clubs?

4. Wolves went out of both domestic cup competitions early on, which was probably just as well considering their Europa League exploits were so draining. They lost to Manchester United in an FA Cup replay, and to Aston Villa at the second hurdle in the League Cup. Who were the only club they won a League Cup tie against, after a penalty shoot-out?

5. Who was the only Wolves player to score in both the Premier League and the League Cup?

6. Two Wolves players saw a red card in the league. Both came in September, the first in a 3-2 defeat at Everton, and the second in a 1-1 draw at Crystal Palace. Which two men got their marching orders?

7. One of the season's highlights was a 2-0 win at Manchester City on 6 October. Who scored both of their goals?

8. On 18 January, Wolves staged a great fightback when they came back from 2-0 down at half time away from home to win 3-2. Who did they beat?

9. Sean Longstaff of Newcastle United, Simon Francis of Bournemouth, Ederson of Manchester City, Christian Kabasele of Watford and Hanza Choudhury of Leicester City. What is the link between these players?

10. He was certainly 'Jonny on the spot' when he scored Wolves' goal in a 1-1 away draw on 27 October. Who were their opponents?

ANSWERS

QUIZ No. 1 ANYTHING GOES - PART 1

1. Neil Emblen – he came from Millwall and the others went to Millwall
2. Harrison, Jones, Mason, Williams and Collins
3. They all came from Aston Villa
4. Lee Evans
5. David Black
6. The Wanderers with five and Bolton Wanderers with four
7. 1956/57
8. Eddie Clamp
9. Steve Kindon – he came from Burnley; the others went to Burnley
10. The Hawthorns

QUIZ No. 2 ANYTHING GOES - PART 2

1. Bury
2. Sheyi Ojo
3. Jay Bothroyd
4. Alan Hinton
5. They were all South Africans
6. All 11 games were home wins
7. Yorkshire
8. Keith Downing
9. One
10. Jack Whitehouse

QUIZ No. 3 ANYTHING GOES - PART 3

1. Tammy Abraham
2. George Showell and Mike Stowell
3. John Ireland
4. Matt Doherty
5. Derek Dougan
6. David Wagstaffe
7. The Leicester player was Ted Jelly and the Spurs player was Martin Chivers, and the latter are jelly makers
8. Stan Cullis
9. Daniel Podence
10. Gray – Andy and Frank

QUIZ No. 4 APPEARANCES

1. Derek Parkin
2. Mark Kendall and Andy Mutch
3. Johnny Hancocks
4. True; Ron Flowers got 49
5. John McAlle
6. Over; 609
7. Tom Galley
8. Alastair Robertson; the club was West Brom
9. Conor Coady
10. Phil Parkes

QUIZ No. 5 ATTENDANCES

1. The 1960 final against Blackburn Rovers
2. Aston Villa
3. Sunderland
4. Anfield
5. 45,000
6. Grimsby Town
7. Highfield Road, Coventry
8. Bloomfield Road, Blackpool
9. Goodison Park
10. Highbury, Arsenal

QUIZ No. 6 AWAY FROM MOLINEUX

1. Derek Mountfield
2. Cyril Sidlow
3. Fred Goodwin
4. Geoff Thomas
5. Hugh McIlmoyle
6. Bob McNab
7. Steve Sedgley
8. Les Smith
9. Alan Sunderland
10. Nigel Sims and Geoff Sidebottom

QUIZ No. 7 CAPITAL CITIES

1. Copenhagen
2. London
3. Belgrade
4. Cardiff
5. Rio de Janeiro
6. Lima
7. Paris
8. Vienna
9. Montevideo
10. Helsinki

QUIZ No. 8 CHRISTMAS CRACKERS

1. Oxford United
2. A 3-3 draw
3. Romain Saiss
4. They lost all four
5. Leicester City
6. 5-3
7. 1962/63
8. 1954/55
9. Manchester United
10. Aston Villa

QUIZ No. 9 CRAZY DAYS

1. Wolves won 6-4
2. 7-4 to Spurs
3. Fulham
4. 5-4
5. Arsenal and Newcastle United
6. Huddersfield Town
7. Chelsea
8. Preston North End
9. Manchester United
10. Arsenal won 5-4

QUIZ No. 10 CRYPTIC WOLVES – PART 1

1. Paul Blades
2. Billy Blunt
3. Geoff Palmer
4. Mark Kendall
5. Terry Springthorpe
6. Mark Venus
7. Bill Shorthouse
8. Ernie Hunt
9. Bob Coy
10. Mark Lazarus

QUIZ No. 11 CRYPTIC WOLVES – PART 2

1. Tom Yule
2. George Lax
3. Willie Carr
4. George Eccles
5. Alf Bishop
6. Johannes De Wolf
7. George Berry
8. Paul Bradshaw
9. Bert Williams
10. Jesus San Juan Garcia

QUIZ No. 12 DYNAMIC DUOS

1. (b) Holmes and Watson
2. (a) Homer and Simpson
3. (d) Cock and Bull
4. (c) Stanley and Matthews
5. (a) Barker and Corbett
6. (b) Mills and Boon
7. (d) Preston and Sunderland
8. (d) Goodman and Crook
9. (c) Nightingale and Pheasant
10. (a) George and Harrison

QUIZ No. 13 FA CUP FINALS

1. Preston North End in 1889
2. Jesse Pye and Norman Deeley
3. All four goals in the game were scored by players whose surname began with the same letter; Hunt, Hedley and Harrison for Wolves and Howie for Newcastle United
4. Dickie Dorsett
5. Barry Stobart
6. 1939
7. True
8. Harry Allen
9. Don Revie
10. 1921 Wolves v Spurs, when Wolves were in Division Two and Spurs were in the Southern League

QUIZ No. 14 FANS

1. Eric Idle
2. Jacqui Oatley
3. Edward Elgar
4. Robert Plant
5. 8,300
6. Ashton Gate, home of Bristol City
7. Punjabi Wolves
8. Suzi Perry
9. Dave Worton
10. Oxford United with *Raging Bull* and Hereford United with *Talking Bull*

QUIZ No. 15 FIRSTS AND LASTS

1. It was an own goal
2. Jackery Jones
3. Dennis Westcott
4. Roy Swinbourne
5. Geoff Palmer

6. Michael Branch
7. Lee Naylor
8. Steve Sedgley
9. Robbie Dennison
10. Matt Doherty

QUIZ No. 16
GOALKEEPERS - PART 1

1. Tim Flowers
2. John Burridge
3. Dave Beasant
4. Malcolm Finlayson
5. Jim Barron
6. Mike Stowell
7. Mark Kendall
8. Phil Parkes
9. Paul Bradshaw
10. Billy Rose

QUIZ No. 17 GOALKEEPERS - PART 2

1. Tommy Lunn
2. 24
3. Fred Davies
4. John and Jack Ruddy
5. Wayne Hennessy
6. Michael Oakes
7. Paul Jones
8. Matt Murray
9. Carl Ikeme
10. Noel George

QUIZ No. 18 HAT-TRICKS - PART 1

1. Ade Akinbiyi
2. David Connolly
3. Darren and Iwan Roberts
4. Roy Swinbourne
5. Bobby Woodruff
6. Jimmy Murray
7. Colin Booth
8. Dennis Westcott
9. Charlie Phillips and Tommy Phillipson
10. Teddy Pheasant

QUIZ No. 19 HAT-TRICKS - PART 2

1. Billy Hartill
2. Johnny Hancocks
3. Micky Lill
4. Terry Wharton
5. Dennis Wilshaw

6. Johannes De Wolf
7. Hugh Curran
8. Steve Bull
9. Nouha Dicko
10. Bobby Gould

QUIZ No. 20 HORRIBLE HAMMERINGS

1. Chelsea
2. Blackpool
3. Arsenal
4. Sunderland
5. Derby County
6. 10-3
7. Newton Heath
8. Southampton
9. Fulham
10. Newcastle United and Middlesbrough

QUIZ No. 21 INTERNATIONALS - ENGLAND

1. Dennis Wilshaw
2. Three
3. Matt Jarvis
4. Peter Broadbent
5. The USA
6. Ron Flowers
7. Bobby Thomson
8. Chris Crowe and John Richards
9. Steve Bull
10. Bill Slater

QUIZ No. 22 INTERNATIONALS - SCOTLAND AND WALES

1. Ipswich Town
2. George Berry
3. Jim McCalliog
4. Paul Jones and Wayne Hennessy
5. Frank Munro
6. Sam Vokes
7. Steven Fletcher
8. Dave Edwards
9. Andy Gray
10. They both got 52 caps

QUIZ No. 23 INTERNATIONALS - THE TWO IRELANDS

1. Robbie Dennison
2. Darren Potter
3. Johnny Gorman

4. Mick Kearns
5. Mark Clyde
6. Kevin Foley
7. Derek Dougan
8. Maurice Daly
9. Peter McParland
10. Steve Hunt

QUIZ No. 24 INTERNATIONALS – OTHER COUNTRIES

1. Portugal
2. Mexico
3. New Zealand
4. Belgium
5. Iceland
6. Serbia
7. Nigeria
8. South Korea
9. Norway
10. Australia

QUIZ No. 25 LEAGUE CUP FINALS

1. Kenny Hibbitt and John Richards
2. Dave Wagstaffe was replaced by Barry Powell
3. Alan Sunderland and Denis Law
4. Phil Parkes
5. Dave Needham and Peter Shilton
6. Emlyn Hughes
7. Mike Bailey
8. Swindon Town
9. Willie Carr
10. Derek Dougan

QUIZ No. 26 LEGENDS NO. 1 – STEVE BULL

1. Cardiff City
2. Hartlepool United
3. Cheltenham Town
4. Birmingham City
5. Notts County
6. Wrexham
7. Scotland at Hampden Park
8. Nine
9. Bradford City
10. Santos of Brazil

QUIZ No. 27 LEGENDS NO. 2 – STAN CULLIS

1. None
2. 900
3. Albert Stubbins
4. Norway
5. Ted Vizard
6. The long-ball game
7. True
8. Andy Beattie
9. Birmingham City
10. 422 – they scored over 100 goals in each of these seasons.

QUIZ No. 28 LEGENDS NO. 3 – DEREK DOUGAN

1. Portsmouth
2. He posted a transfer request on the morning of the final
3. Nottingham Forest
4. Hull City and Manchester City
5. 43
6. Leicester City
7. Peterborough United
8. False – 95 for Wolves and 127 for the others
9. Middlesbrough and FC Porto
10. Chairman and chief executive

QUIZ No. 29 LEGENDS NO. 4 – RON FLOWERS

1. Doncaster
2. He scored, but Wolves lost 5-2
3. Chelsea
4. It was England's first-ever goal in the European Championship
5. Newcastle United
6. Billy Wright
7. Aston Villa
8. He was told that he would be playing in the World Cup Final the next day if Jack Charlton didn't shake off the illness which he was suffering from
9. Portsmouth
10. Northampton Town

QUIZ No. 30 LEGENDS NO. 5 – SIR JACK HAYWARD

1. 1990
2. 17
3. £10, but he had to spend £30 million on the club
4. Life President
5. Surrey and the first Womens' Cricket World Cup
6. Jeremy Thorpe
7. Warm bath and slashing my wrists
8. Sons Jonathan and Rick and grandson Rupert
9. The Jack Harris Stand
10. Molineux Way

QUIZ No. 31 LEGENDS NO. 6 – KENNY HIBBITT

1. Chelsea
2. Wales
3. 17
4. Hillsborough, in 1981, against Spurs
5. He and his brother Terry, who was playing for Newcastle United, scored both of the goals in the game
6. True
7. Everton
8. Newcastle United
9. Luton Town
10. Bristol Rovers

QUIZ No. 32 LEGENDS NO. 7 – BILLY WRIGHT

1. Highbury, Stamford Bridge and White Hart Lane
2. Nottingham Forest
3. Number Six
4. Charlton Athletic
5. 90
6. Sheffield United and Sunderland
7. Scotland
8. Joy Beverly
9. Arsenal
10. 70

QUIZ No. 33 MANAGERS – PART 1

1. Paul Lambert
2. Brian Little and Dean Saunders
3. Mick McCarthy
4. Terry Connor
5. Norway
6. Graham Turner
7. Walter Zenga
8. Bill McGarry
9. John Addenbrooke
10. Graham Hawkins

QUIZ No. 34 – MANAGERS – PART 2

1. Kenny Jackett
2. Major Frank Buckley
3. Glenn Hoddle and Graham Taylor
4. Ronnie Allen and Tommy Docherty
5. Sammy Chung and Sammy Chapman
6. John Barnwell
7. Goalkeeper
8. Colin Lee
9. Stan Cullis
10. Mark McGhee

QUIZ No. 35 MOLINEUX

1. Dudley Road
2. Notts County
3. An FA Cup semi-final
4. Liverpool
5. The Molineux Street Stand
6. Scotland
7. Denmark
8. Tommy Taylor
9. The Billy Wright Stand
10. The Steve Bull Stand

QUIZ No. 36 MULTIPLE CHOICE – PART 1

1. (a) Mansfield Town
2. (d) Policeman
3. (b) Jehovah's Witnesses
4. (c) Hiroshima Antlers
5. (d) 99
6. (b) Jimmy Mullen
7. (a) third
8. (d) Evan
9. (d) 14-0
10. (a) Liverpool

QUIZ No. 37 MULTIPLE CHOICE - PART 2

1. (a) Flipper
2. (d) Church
3. (a) Darren Ferguson
4. (b) Jimmy Greaves
5. (c) Leicester City
6. (b) Chard, 1988/89
7. (d) Cardiff City
8. (a) Lillie Bridge
9. (d) Portsmouth
10. (c) 1949/50

QUIZ No. 38 OCCUPATIONAL WOLVES

1. Joe Butcher
2. Paul Cook
3. Ted Farmer and Jimmy Greaves
4. Albert Fletcher and Tom Hunter
5. Mason
6. Paul Butler
7. Billy Crook
8. Tom Knight
9. Bill Slater
10. Cutler; the players were Eric and Reg

QUIZ No. 39 OPENING DAY

1. Lincoln City
2. Manchester City
3. Arsenal
4. Jimmy Murray
5. Nottingham Forest
6. Ted Farmer
7. Bramall Lane
8. Grimsby Town
9. Sam Vokes
10. Robbie Keane

QUIZ No. 40 OTHER COMPETITIONS

1. 4-4
2. The Texaco Cup
3. They won all four away games, but only one at home
4. The Freight-Rover Trophy
5. Burnley by 2-0
6. Steve Bull
7. Torquay United
8. The Zenith Data Systems Cup
9. The Anglo-Italian Cup
10. The Watney Cup

QUIZ No. 41 PLAY-OFFS AND PENALTY SHOOT-OUTS

1. Arsenal
2. Aldershot
3. Bolton Wanderers
4. Crystal Palace
5. Norwich City
6. Sheffield United; Kennedy, Blake and Miller
7. Leicester City
8. Sheffield Wednesday
9. Burnley
10. Chesterfield

QUIZ No. 42 POLITICAL WOLVES

1. Eric Nixon
2. Derek Jefferson
3. Jackie Brown
4. Les Wilson
5. Colin Cameron
6. Mark Kennedy
7. Andy Blair
8. Gary Pierce
9. Stacey North
10. Roger Johnson

QUIZ No. 43 QUOTES

1. Mike Bailey
2. Graham Turner
3. Tommy Docherty
4. Henri Camara
5. Mick McCarthy
6. Dave Jones
7. Andy Gray
8. Paul Ince
9. Sir Jack Hayward
10. Sir Alex Ferguson

QUIZ No. 44 SUBLIME SCORES

1. Manchester City
2. Ashton Gate
3. Preston North End, Mansfield Town and Gillingham
4. Chelsea
5. Portsmouth
6. Huddersfield Town
7. Fulham
8. Cardiff City

9. Burnley
10. Everton

QUIZ No. 45 TRANSFERS – 1888-1939

1. Southampton
2. Archie Goodall
3. Bryn Jones
4. Billy Harrison
5. Tommy Phillipson
6. Alf Tootill
7. Everton
8. Chelsea
9. Burnley
10. Tom Baddeley

QUIZ No. 46 TRANSFERS 1945-59

1. Walsall
2. West Ham United
3. Peter Broadbent and Bill Slater, the latter returned there
4. Jesse Pye
5. Colin Booth
6. Dennis Westcott
7. Grimsby Town
8. Stoke City
9. Aston Villa
10. Derby County

QUIZ No. 47 TRANSFERS – THE 1960s

1. Bradford Park Avenue
2. Crystal Palace
3. Ray Crawford
4. Nottingham Forest and Derby County
5. Alun Evans
6. Terry Wharton
7. Jimmy Melia
8. Jimmy Murray and Barry Stobart
9. David Burnside
10. Walsall

QUIZ No. 48 TRANSFERS – THE 1970s

1. Mike O'Grady
2. Minnesota Kicks
3. Hugh Curran
4. Bobby Gould
5. Peter Withe
6. Bob Hazell

7. Dave Thomas
8. Watford
9. Peter Daniel
10. Rotherham United

QUIZ No. 49 TRANSFERS – THE 1980s

1. Alan Ainscow
2. Danny Crainie
3. Andy Mutch
4. Norman Bell
5. Wayne Clark
6. John Humphrey
7. Mel Eves
8. Andy King
9. They all went abroad, Richards to Maritimo Funchal, Bradshaw to Vancouver Whitecaps and Brazier to Jacksonville Teamen
10. Floyd Streete

QUIZ No. 50 TRANSFERS – THE 1990s

1. Paul Birch
2. Mark Rankine
3. Dean Richards
4. Robert Neistroj and Haavard Flo
5. Geoff Thomas
6. David Kelly
7. Andy Thompson
8. Peter Shirtliff
9. Mark Burke
10. Lawrie Madden

QUIZ No. 51 TRANSFERS – THE 2000s

1. Gary Breen, Paul Butler, Neil Collins, Jody Craddock, Stephen Elliott, Greg Halford and Alex Rae
2. Blackburn Rovers
3. Middlesbrough
4. Stoke City
5. Charlton Athletic
6. Coventry City
7. Kenny Miller
8. Ronald Zubar
9. Wimbledon and Crystal Palace
10. Jackie McNamara and Charlie Mulgrew

QUIZ No. 52 TRANSFERS – THE 2010s

1. Sporting Lisbon
2. Porto
3. Anderlecht
4. Atletico Madrid
5. Monaco
6. Benfica
7. Angers
8. Lillestrom
9. Heerenveen
10. Legia Warsaw

QUIZ No. 53 TRUE OR FALSE – PART 1

1. False; it was two seasons
2. True; 45 to 22
3. True
4. False; Leicester City got 102 points in 2013/14
5. True
6. False; the score is correct but the match was switched to Molineux after Wolves gave Reading £450
7. True
8. True
9. True
10. True; the winners were Emlyn Hughes and Andy Gray

QUIZ No. 54 TRUE OR FALSE – PART 2

1. True
2. False; Bill Slater played as an amateur for Blackpool in the 1951 FA Cup Final
3. False; Denis Law scored for Manchester United in the 1963 final
4. False; it was cricket not rugby
5. True
6. False
7. True
8. True
9. True
10. True

QUIZ No. 55 TRUE OR FALSE – PART 3

1. True
2. True; Clamp, Wright and Slater

3. True
4. True
5. True
6. False; Nottingham Forest also did it
7. False; Harry Wood also played in all those finals
8. True
9. True
10. False; Ronald Zubar played in 2009/10

QUIZ No. 56 UNDER THE MOLINEUX LIGHTS

1. George Best
2. Yankee Stadium, New York City
3. Lev Yashin
4. Racing Club of Buenos Aires and Maccabi of Tel Aviv
5. 4-0
6. Ferenc Puskas
7. Roy Swinbourne
8. Chelsea
9. The *Daily Mirror*
10. Glenn Hoddle

QUIZ No. 57 VENUES

1. The Hawthorns
2. Perry Barr
3. Old Trafford
4. Stamford Bridge
5. Hillsborough
6. Leeds Road, Huddersfield
7. The Baseball Ground, Derby
8. Kennington Oval
9. Highbury
10. Maine Road

QUIZ No. 58 WHO AM I?

1. Gordon Cowans
2. Temur Ketsbaia
3. Adama Traore
4. Robbie Keane
5. Neil Masters
6. Ade Akinbiyi
7. Jack Dowen
8. Morgan Gibbs-White
9. Jack Rowley
10. Chic Brodie

QUIZ No. 59 WOLVES AGAINST LANCASHIRE CLUBS

1. Burnley
2. Preston North End
3. Bury
4. Blackburn Rovers
5. Accrington
6. Bolton Wanderers
7. Blackpool
8. Oldham Athletic
9. Rochdale
10. Wigan Athletic

QUIZ No. 60 WOLVES AGAINST LONDON CLUBS

1. QPR
2. Leyton Orient
3. Fulham
4. Arsenal and Chelsea
5. Spurs
6. Brentford
7. Crystal Palace
8. Charlton Athletic
9. Millwall
10. West Ham United

QUIZ No. 61 WOLVES AGAINST MIDLANDS CLUBS (EXCLUDING WEST BROMWICH ALBION)

1. Coventry City
2. Birmingham City
3. Leicester City
4. Notts County
5. Stoke City
6. Derby County and Aston Villa
7. True
8. Nottingham Forest
9. Northampton Town
10. Long Eaton Rangers

QUIZ No. 62 WOLVES AGAINST YORKSHIRE CLUBS

1. Sheffield Wednesday
2. Huddersfield Town
3. Doncaster Rovers
4. Bradford City
5. Sheffield United
6. Hull City
7. Leeds United
8. True
9. Rotherham United
10. Barnsley

QUIZ No. 63 WOLVES BARING TEETH (SENDINGS-OFF)

1. Tom Baddeley
2. Steve Bull
3. Willy Bolly
4. Alex Scott
5. Danny Hegan and John Richards
6. Andy Gray
7. Highbury
8. Ewood Park
9. He was the first player to have an actual red card waved at him
10. Paul Butler

QUIZ No. 64 WOLVES IN EUROPE - 1958-80

1. Schalke 04
2. Peter Broadbent
3. Mike Bailey
4. Locomotiv Leipzig
5. Glasgow Rangers
6. Portugal, Holland, Germany, Italy and Hungary
7. Derek Dougan scored one of the goals, but the other three were all own goals
8. PSV Eindhoven
9. Mel Eves
10. Barcelona, Porto, Juventus, PSV Eindhoven and Red Star Belgrade

QUIZ No. 65 WOLVES IN THE EUROPA LEAGUE - 2019/20

1. Crusaders
2. Ryan Bennett
3. 4-0
4. Torino
5. Raul Jimenez
6. Willy Bolly
7. Diogo Jota
8. Leander Dendoncker
9. Espanyol and Olympiacos
10. Seville

QUIZ No. 66 WOLVES IN THE FA CUP - 1883-1915

1. Old Carthusians
2. Jack Brodie

3. Derby St Luke's
4. Aston Villa
5. Blackburn Rovers
6. Derby County
7. Southampton and Sunderland
8. Sheffield Wednesday
9. 1893 and 1908
10. Crystal Palace and Chelsea

QUIZ No. 67 WOLVES IN THE FA CUP - 1919-39

1. Cardiff City
2. Fulham
3. Liverpool; at Goodison Park in round four and Anfield in the semi-final
4. Mansfield Town
5. Wrexham
6. Arsenal
7. Hull City
8. Sunderland
9. Dennis Westcott
10. Preston North End 3 Wolves 0 – 1889 final repeated score in 1922 and Sheffield Wednesday 2 Wolves 1 – 1896 final repeated score in 1935

QUIZ No. 68 WOLVES IN THE FA CUP - 1945-60

1. Lovells Athletic
2. Sheffield United
3. Manchester United
4. Sheffield; Bramall Lane in round four and Hillsborough in the semi-final
5. Blackpool
6. Bournemouth
7. Bolton Wanderers
8. Sammy Smyth and Norman Deeley
9. Plymouth Argyle
10. Mick McGrath and Dave Whelan

QUIZ No. 69 WOLVES IN CUP COMPETITIONS - THE 1960s

1. Fulham and QPR
2. Huddersfield Town
3. Spurs
4. Dave Wagstaffe, Terry Wharton, Frank Wignall, Les Wilson, Dave Woodfield and Bobby Woodruff
5. Manchester United
6. West Brom
7. Altrincham
8. Hugh McIlmoyle
9. Southend, Blackpool and Brighton
10. Rotherham United

QUIZ No. 70 WOLVES IN CUP COMPETITIONS - THE 1970s

1. Oxford United
2. Norwich City
3. They didn't concede a goal
4. Leeds United
5. Ipswich Town
6. Arsenal
7. Liverpool
8. Mansfield Town
9. 11
10. Grimsby Town at the Baseball Ground, Derby

QUIZ No. 71 WOLVES IN CUP COMPETITIONS - THE 1980s

1. Willie Carr and Kenny Hibbitt
2. Wrexham
3. 14
4. Aston Villa
5. Walsall
6. Lincoln City
7. Coventry City
8. Chorley
9. Burnden Park, Bolton
10. Steve Bull

QUIZ No. 72 WOLVES IN CUP COMPETITIONS - THE 1990s

1. Cambridge United and Hull City
2. 6-1
3. Aston Villa
4. Watford, Wimbledon and Wigan Athletic
5. Mixu Paatelainen
6. Swindon Town
7. Barnet
8. Arsenal
9. Charlton Athletic
10. Sheffield Wednesday

QUIZ No. 73 WOLVES IN THE LEAGUE - 1888-1915

1. Aston Villa and West Brom
2. Third, in 1888/89 and 1897/98
3. Bury and Bolton Wanderers
4. Harry Wood and Billy Wooldridge
5. Roker Park, Sunderland
6. 1905/06
7. Gainsborough Trinity and Glossop North End
8. Wolves had won eight games in a row and Birmingham stopped their run
9. Fourth
10. Stockport County

QUIZ No. 74 WOLVES IN THE LEAGUE - 1919-39

1. The Hawthorns
2. October
3. None
4. Stoke City
5. 71
6. Arsenal and Everton
7. True
8. Sunderland
9. Blackpool
10. True

QUIZ No. 75 WOLVES IN THE LEAGUE - 1946-60

1. 5-1
2. Portsmouth
3. West Brom
4. Billy Wright
5. Eight
6. Manchester United
7. Jimmy Murray
8. Arsenal
9. Newcastle United
10. Dennis Westcott

QUIZ No. 76 WOLVES IN THE LEAGUE - 1960s

1. Arsenal
2. Spurs and Fulham
3. Derek Parkin
4. Ray Crawford and Derek Dougan
5. Birmingham City
6. Portsmouth
7. Crystal Palace
8. Nottingham Forest
9. 13
10. Terry Wharton

QUIZ No. 77 WOLVES IN THE LEAGUE - 1970s

1. 22
2. Derek Dougan and Frank Munro
3. Bobby Gould
4. Emlyn Hughes
5. QPR
6. Hereford United and Bristol Rovers
7. John Richards
8. Geoff Palmer, Derek Parkin, Gary Pierce and Steve Daley
9. Hugh Curran
10. Sheffield United and Burnley

QUIZ No. 78 WOLVES IN THE LEAGUE - 1980s

1. John Humphrey
2. John Burridge and Paul Bradshaw
3. Steve Mardenborough
4. Five
5. Mel Eves
6. 33
7. 34
8. Andy Mutch
9. Steve Bull scored hat-tricks against them, getting four against Preston North End
10. Bristol Rovers

QUIZ No. 79 WOLVES IN THE LEAGUE - 1990s

1. 19
2. David Holdsworth
3. Andy Mutch
4. The Stadium of Light, Sunderland
5. Robbie Keane
6. Keith Curle
7. Dougie Freedman
8. Paul Birch, Mark Burke, Tom Bennett and Gary Bellamy
9. Daley Thompson; the players were Tony Daley and Andy Thompson
10. Tranmere Rovers

QUIZ No. 80 WOLVES VERSUS WEST BROMWICH ALBION

1. Jimmy Mullen
2. It relegated West Brom
3. Jay Bothroyd
4. Five
5. They all played over 100 games for each club
6. 7-0
7. 3-3
8. Steve Bull
9. Robbie Dennison
10. It was the first season that they had met in the two league games where no goals had been scored in either game

QUIZ No. 81 WOLVES – SEASON 2000/01

1. Timour Ketsbaia
2. Steve Claridge
3. George Ndah
4. Nottingham Forest
5. Oxford United
6. Michael Oakes and Kevin Naylor
7. Wycombe Wanderers
8. Adam Proudlock and Carl Robinson
9. Andy Sinton and Steve Sedgley
10. Joleon Lescott

QUIZ No. 82 WOLVES – SEASON 2001/02

1. West Brom and Birmingham City
2. Portsmouth
3. Gillingham
4. Dean Sturridge
5. Tony Dinning
6. Bradford City
7. Manchester City
8. 3-0
9. Alex Rae
10. Colin Cooper

QUIZ No. 83 WOLVES – SEASON 2002/03

1. 76
2. Dougie Freedman
3. Sheffield Wednesday and Ipswich Town
4. Kenny Miller

5. Gillingham
6. One
7. Reading
8. George Ndah
9. Denis Irwin and Joleon Lescott
10. Groundsman of the Year

QUIZ No. 84 WOLVES – SEASON 2003/04

1. Morecambe
2. Leicester City and Leeds United
3. Stefan Iversen
4. Colin Cameron
5. Henri Camara
6. Kidderminster Harriers
7. Kevin Naylor
8. West Ham United and Arsenal
9. Jody Craddock
10. Robbie Keane

QUIZ No. 85 WOLVES – SEASON 2004/05

1. Dave Jones was sacked and replaced with Glenn Hoddle
2. Colin Cameron
3. Keith Lowe
4. Sheffield United
5. They were all 1-1 draws
6. Millwall and Arsenal
7. Rochdale and Burnley
8. Ki-Hyeon Seol
9. 21
10. Mikkel Bischoff and Rohan Ricketts

QUIZ No. 86 WOLVES – SEASON 2005/06

1. Glenn Hoddle
2. Carl Cort
3. Tom Huddlestone
4. Plymouth Argyle
5. Paul Ince
6. Joleon Lescott
7. Kenny Miller
8. Jeremie Aliadiere
9. Viorel Ganea
10. Darren Anderton

QUIZ No. 87 WOLVES - SEASON 2006/07

1. Sunderland
2. Jay Bothroyd
3. Leon Clarke
4. Jody Craddock
5. Chris Iwelumo
6. Kevin Phillips
7. Michael Kightly
8. Seyi Olofinjana
9. Matt Murray
10. Leicester City

QUIZ No. 88 WOLVES - SEASON 2007/08

1. Watford
2. Neil Collins
3. Wolves beat Cardiff City and lost to Crystal Palace
4. Plymouth Argyle
5. Andy Keogh
6. Karl Henry
7. Seyi Olofinjana
8. Scunthorpe United
9. Bradford City
10. Wayne Hennessy

QUIZ No. 89 WOLVES - SEASON 2008/09

1. Seven
2. QPR
3. Kyel Reid
4. Wayne Hennessy and Carl Ikeme
5. Kevin Foley
6. Norwich City and Preston North End
7. Sam Vokes
8. Accrington Stanley
9. Birmingham City and Burnley
10. Richard Stearman

QUIZ No. 90 WOLVES - SEASON 2009/10

1. Reading
2. Wigan Athletic
3. Spurs and Burnley
4. Jody Craddock and Ronald Zubar
5. He put out a reserve team
6. Marcus Hahnemann
7. Matt Jarvis
8. Clarke Carlisle

9. Karl Henry
10. Adlene Guedioura

QUIZ No. 91 WOLVES - SEASON 2010/11

1. One
2. Stephen Ward
3. Jose Bosingwa
4. Doncaster Rovers
5. Stoke City
6. Manchester City; the brothers were Kolo and Ya Ya Toure
7. Blackpool
8. Wigan Athletic
9. Richard Stearman
10. Kevin Doyle

QUIZ No. 92 WOLVES - SEASON 2011/12

1. Second, after winning their first two games
2. Bolton Wanderers and Blackburn Rovers
3. Millwall
4. Old Trafford, The Emirates and St James' Park
5. Birmingham City
6. Swansea City
7. Steven Fletcher
8. Wayne Hennessy
9. West Brom and Manchester United
10. Mick McCarthy

QUIZ No. 93 WOLVES - SEASON 2012/13

1. Bristol City
2. Birmingham City
3. Luton Town
4. Northampton Town
5. Sylvan Ebanks-Blake
6. Stale Solbakken and Dean Saunders
7. Tom Ince
8. Roger Johnson
9. Benik Afobe
10. Bakary Sako

QUIZ No. 94 WOLVES - SEASON 2013/14

1. 103
2. Kenny Jackett

3. Leyton Orient
4. Nine
5. Sam Ricketts
6. Carnoustie
7. Oldham Athletic and Morecambe
8. 6-4 to Wolves
9. Leigh Griffiths
10. Walsall

QUIZ No. 95 WOLVES - SEASON 2014/15

1. Brentford and Ipswich Town
2. Bakary Sako
3. Five
4. True; 45 from the start plus one sub
5. Nouha Dicko
6. Arsenal
7. Leeds United and Dave Edwards
8. Conor Coady
9. Millwall and Reading
10. Rotherham United

QUIZ No. 96 WOLVES - SEASON 2015/16

1. Seven
2. Blackburn Rovers
3. Newport County and Barnet
4. Adam Le Fondre
5. Michal Zyro
6. Matt Doherty
7. False; Afobe was top scorer with nine
8. Dominic Iorfa
9. Danny Batth
10. West Ham United

QUIZ No. 97 WOLVES - SEASON 2016/17

1. Kenny Jackett, Walter Zenga and Paul Lambert
2. Five
3. Joao Teixeira
4. Helder Costa and Ivan Cavaleiro
5. Barnsley
6. Joe Mason
7. Crawley Town and Cambridge United
8. Brentford and Fulham
9. Anders Weimann
10. Chelsea

QUIZ No. 98 WOLVES - SEASON 2017/18

1. Nottingham Forest
2. Leo Bonatini
3. Diogo Jota
4. Bolton Wanderers
5. Leeds United
6. Yeovil Town, Southampton and Bristol Rovers
7. Alfred N'Diaye
8. They missed two penalties in the last few minutes
9. Will Norris
10. Ruben Neves and Willy Boly

QUIZ No. 99 WOLVES - SEASON 2018/19

1. Jamie Vardy
2. Adama Traore
3. Conor Coady
4. Sheffield Wednesday
5. Manchester United
6. 4-3 to Wolves
7. Matt Doherty
8. Leander Dendoncker
9. Deandre Yedlin
10. Bristol City

QUIZ No. 100 WOLVES - SEASON 2019/20

1. True
2. Rui Patricio and Conor Coady
3. Aston Villa, Bournemouth, West Ham United, Norwich City and Manchester City
4. Reading
5. Patrick Cutrone
6. Willy Boly and Romain Saiss
7. Adama Traore
8. Southampton
9. They were all sent off against Wolves in the league
10. Newcastle United

From the introduction, the five drinks companies are The Milk Marketing Board, Coca-Cola, Worthington, Carling and Carabao.